Christian Caring

Christian Caring

Selections from *Practical Theology*

Friedrich Schleiermacher

Edited with an Introduction by
James O. Duke and Howard Stone
Translated by James O. Duke

Contents

Editors' Preface 7

Schleiermacher's
Practical Theology

An Orientation by James Duke and Howard Stone 13

    Practical Theology and the Ministry of the Church 13

    The Study of Theology 16

    The Field of Practical Theology 24

    Special Pastoral Care 33

Translator's Note 45

Selected Bibliography 48

Practical Theology: Selections
by Friedrich Schleiermacher

Special Pastoral Care, or Pastoral Care in the Strict Sense 53

Introduction to the Field 82

Editors' Preface

In recent years the relationship between theology and the practice of ministry has again become a topic of lively conversation in churches and seminaries. The common concern is that the relationship be as clear and productive as possible. The challenges facing the ministry of the church in our times would seem to demand nothing less. Not surprisingly there has also been a revival of interest in practical theology and, likewise, a great deal of fresh study about the story of theological education. This book dealing with Friedrich Schleiermacher's thoughts about practical theology as Christian caring is a natural outcome of these interests.

These thoughts are worth considering today because Schleiermacher (1768–1834), often called "the founder of modern theology," was also a pioneer, with strikingly contemporary concerns, in the field of practical theology. He wanted to clarify the relationship between the study of theology and the ministry of the church, and as a result he urged that a theology of the practice of ministry receive special attention. It did in his own teaching career. He was the first to set forth a vision of practical theology as a unified field of study integral to theological education by delineating its aim, its scope, and its elements. In all that he did, he was guided by the conviction that the ministry of the church was best served by a practical theology that was at once academically sound and practically relevant. The strengths, and limits, of his vision provide a fitting point of departure for anyone who cares about the future of practical theology, theological education, and the ministry of the church.

The present book is a joint enterprise by a pastoral theologian, Howard Stone, and a historical theologian, James Duke. It was conceived quite by accident during a chat at coffee break. Stone had been reading about the theology of pastoral care; Duke, about theological education in nineteenth-century Germany. When the inevitable question came, "What've you been working on?" we surprised each other by answering, "Schleiermacher's practical theology." Stone wondered why, if the book was so important, it had never been translated. Duke was left to wonder why it had been so rarely dealt with even by Schleiermacher specialists. We decided to work together to change the situation.

The collaboration has been beneficial to us, not only because we have learned from each other but because we have found Schleiermacher the practical theologian to be of more than historical interest. He has much to say to seminarians and their instructors, ministers, and church people in general. We have tried to keep this audience, rather than one comprised of nineteenth-century specialists, uppermost in our minds as we went about our work on this project. We have limited references in our annotations, for example, primarily to sources available in English.

The book is in two parts. The first is an orientation to Schleiermacher's thinking about practical theology. It offers some background information about the setting and intention of his thought, an analysis of some of his key concepts, and an exposition of some major points of special interest to contemporary readers. The second part contains a translation of two selections from Schleiermacher's lectures on practical theology, delivered to theology students at the University of Berlin and reconstructed for publication in the posthumous edition of his collected works under the title *Practical Theology, Systematically Presented According to the Principles of the Evangelical Church.*

The two portions included here are the general introduction to practical theology as a whole and the section on pastoral care. The latter has been placed first in this edition so that readers may move directly to the pastoral resources which Schleiermacher offers before stepping back to consider his overall conception of the field of practical theology. The section on pastoral care deals with matters familiar to contemporary ministers. Discussing religious doubts, addressing questions of conscience, responding to scandals and disputes, counseling about divorce, visiting the sick, performing funerals—these are the topics about which this part of practical theology has something to say. In the general introduction Schleiermacher develops his conception of the field in a step-by-step fashion,

Editors' Preface

leading his audience through a series of issues crucial for any attempt to define the aim, character, and organization of practical theology.

Obviously, other selections could have been included. Obviously, too, only a study of all 844 pages of his *Practical Theology* would give a complete picture of Schleiermacher's concerns. These selections, however, serve as a good introduction to his thought, especially because there is a deep bond between them. Schleiermacher said that all of practical theology is a matter of "the care of souls" (*psychologia, Seelsorge*) and he called the task of pastoral care and counseling "the care of souls in the narrow (or strict) sense of the word." These texts call to mind a critical juncture in the history of the field of practical theology. Perhaps they will encourage readers to think about the task of the practical theologian as creatively in our day as Schleiermacher did in his.

Each of us wishes to take this opportunity to express appreciation for kind assistance we have received in the course of our work on this project.

HOWARD STONE: A good portion of this book was written during my research leave from 1985 to 1986. The burden of my teaching and supervising responsibilities during that year was cast on many of my colleagues at Brite Divinity School, especially on Marcus Bryant. I am grateful to Texas Christian University for granting me the leave and to each of my colleagues for carrying the extra load. In addition, I want to express appreciation to the staff and students of Westcott House at Cambridge University for providing such a supportive and conducive setting for my research. Finally, I am grateful for the work that Karen Stone has done in the reading and preparation of portions of the book.

JAMES DUKE: My research for this project, conducted primarily during a research leave in 1984 at the University of Munich, was made possible by Brite Divinity School, the Research Foundation of Texas Christian University, the Younger Scholars Program of the Association of Theological Schools, the Southwest Region of the American Academy of Religion, and Professor Trutz Rendtorff of the Institut für systematische Theologie. I am honored to acknowledge this support. To Dr. Friedrich Graf, who shared with me not only his office and his knowledge of modern theology but his friendship as well, I give many thanks. In addition, I am grateful to Astrid Berger, Albert Blackwell, John Thiel, Charles Wood, and Wilhelm Wuellner who reviewed drafts of the translation. Their suggestions have been invaluable, and they bear no responsibility for any of its shortcomings. Carol Sumner Schneider and Priscilla Stuckey-Kaufmann have been superb research assistants, and Ann Chambers and Audrey Englert deserve commendation for their secretarial services.

SCHLEIERMACHER'S
PRACTICAL THEOLOGY

An Orientation
by James Duke and
Howard Stone

PRACTICAL THEOLOGY AND THE
MINISTRY OF THE CHURCH

Concern runs high these days for a practical theology that contributes to the ministry of the church. It is shared by those who want to serve more effectively in their local congregations, those who want to make a Christian witness for freedom, justice, and reconciliation throughout the world, and perhaps especially those who insist that these two spheres of Christian involvement must go hand in hand. One outgrowth of this concern is an interest in reexamining what is, and should be, going on in theological education. What should we expect the field of practical theology to contribute to the ministry of the church?

Of course, whether practical theology is a field of study is very much an issue in the United States. Preaching, worship, administration, education, and pastoral care are well established in theological schools. These courses or departments, as well as those dealing with spirituality, social action, evangelism, world mission, stewardship, and the like, are commonly grouped together under the heading "practical theology." Each attempts to address some particular aspect of Christian practice—a ministerial task, a church program, a plan for personal development. Those in seminaries spend much time discussing how to balance the "practical" and the "classical" components of their curricula.

Yet the unity of the field of practical theology and its proper relationship to the other theological disciplines, on the one hand, and to the ministry of the church, on the other, remain unsettled. It is frequently thought of as a bridge between academic theory and life practice. But since the time of Aristotle the proper connection between theory and practice has itself been the subject of much debate, and perhaps never more so than in the present.[1] Practical theology finds itself in something of a Catch-22. It is pressured to attend ever more carefully to skills, techniques, methods, and programs even as it is reminded to keep abreast of the "theories" taught in biblical studies, church history, and theology. If the field in genuinely practical, how can it be theological? If it is genuinely theological, how can it be practical?

If you were to look up "Practical Theology" in the card catalog of your seminary library, chances are that you would find few listings other than cross-references to this or that specialty. In the United States, studies that cover practical theology as a whole are only now once again coming into their own. Its integrity as a branch of theological study, its overall purpose, and its principle of organization—these are topics currently under reexamination.[2]

In such a situation it is worthwhile to consider the first thorough, and searching, examination which they received. Early in the nineteenth century Friedrich Schleiermacher—pastor, theologian, activist for social-political and educational reform—committed himself to setting practical theology on a new footing within theological education and the church.

His commitment reflected sensitivities growing out of his life experiences.[3] He was born on November 21, 1768, in Breslau, Silesia. His father was a military chaplain representing the Reformed (Calvinist) church; his mother, the daughter of a minister. Due to the pietistic leanings of his father, Schleiermacher was schooled under the direction of the "Herrnhütter" or Moravian Brethren. The intensity of Christian feeling within this community was a lasting influence upon him. His coming of age, however, was a time of personal turmoil marked by religious doubt and vocational uncertainty, especially as he confronted the world of modern science, philosophy, and literature. Relations with his father were for a time seriously strained, and it was in large measure due to the encouragement of his uncle, Samuel Stubenrauch, an Enlightenment-oriented professor of Reformed theology at Halle, that Schleiermacher eventually completed his university education at Halle, passed his theological examinations (with difficulty only in dogmatics!), and entered the ministry.

The year 1797 found him in Berlin, as the Reformed chaplain at the Charité Hospital. A center of intellectual and social life, Berlin offered Schleiermacher the opportunity to expand his horizons, and he became a member of the talented circle of romantics that had formed there. *On Religion: Speeches to Its Cultured Despisers*, the book that first brought him to popular attention, offered a new style of religious apologetics, and like his next work, *Soliloquies*, was composed in a romantic key.[4]

After leaving Berlin in 1802, Schleiermacher served in the parish. He also pressed forward with his work on the translation of Plato, a project which was initiated during his association with Friedrich Schlegel in Berlin and eventually resulted in a widely acclaimed multivolume edition. In 1804 he was appointed lecturer and university preacher at the University of Halle. There he taught biblical exegesis, dogmatics, ethics, and hermeneutics, and published *Christmas Eve*, a meditation on the meaning of Christmas cast in the form of a modern-day Platonic dialogue.[5] The stay in Halle, however, was abruptly cut short when, in 1806, Napoleon's invasion of German territory forced the closure of the university.

Schleiermacher returned to Berlin, where he lectured, wrote, and actively campaigned on behalf of the Prussian resistance effort against Napoleon and for social and political reforms designed to promote freedom, democracy, and civil rights. His article "Occasional Thoughts about Universities in the German Sense" (1808), written amidst discussions about the establishment of a new university in Berlin, spoke out for academic freedom, high scholarly standards, and a broad liberal education.[6] In association with the Prussian Ministry of Education, he was able to play a significant part in the formation of the new institution.[7] In 1809 he married Henriette von Willich, the young widow of a friend, who had been left with one small child and another on the way.

In that same year he became minister at Trinity Church, and shortly thereafter was named professor of theology (and first dean of the faculty) at the new University of Berlin. The remainder of his life was filled with teaching, research, and pastoral responsibilities. His most significant publication was his dogmatics, *The Christian Faith*.[8] But his courses covered a wide spectrum of theological disciplines (except Old Testament!) as well as such philosophical topics as dialectics (philosophical foundations), aesthetics, pedagogy, ethics, hermeneutics, and psychology.[9] Active in church affairs, he advocated greater lay participation in church government, the union of Lutheran and Reformed churches in Prussia, and less rigid use of creedal tests of orthodoxy. Throughout his life he remained a progressive in the church—and in politics—despite the dangers of displeasing authorities in Prussia who, after the Congress of Vienna (1814), turned away from reformist policies in favor of their more typical conservatism.

Schleiermacher's age, like our own, was one of intellectual, cultural, and social ferment. Forces of revolution and reaction, each in its own way critical of the status quo, insisted that theological education (and much else, of course) be "reformed." Schleiermacher entered into the controversy with a bold reconception of the study of theology as a whole. His proposal, a "formal theological encyclopedia" setting forth a grand design of the aim, elements, and organization of "theological science,"came out under the modest title *Brief Outline of the Study of Theology*.[10] In it, practical theology took its place as the culminating moment of the theological enterprise. So great was his commitment to the field that Schleiermacher lectured on the subject six times in the course of his teaching career at the University of Berlin.

Over the years many theologians have used Schleiermacher's views, especially those expounded in the *Brief Outline*, as a point of departure for their own proposals to reform theological education. True to its name, however, the book is short and sketchy, and nowhere more so than in the section on practical theology. To gain a proper understanding of Schleiermacher's conception of the field, one must go beyond the *Brief Outline* to his lectures on the subject.

The set of these lectures, reconstructed partly from Schleiermacher's own notes and partly from those of his students, has become in Germany a classic in the field,[11] all too often inaccessible to or overlooked by people in other lands. That is unfortunate, for Schleiermacher the practical theologian invites thoughtful and committed Christians—seminarians, pastors, scholars, and anyone else with interest—to sharpen their thinking about the bond between ministerial practice and theological reflection. His own thinking quite naturally starts with a practical issue facing those like himself who are supposed to offer students preparing for ministry a "theological education": what sort of business are we about?

THE STUDY OF THEOLOGY

The aim, unity, and organization of theological science were worked out with considerable methodological sophistication in the *Brief Outline*. In it Schleiermacher reminds us not to forget the obvious: practical theology is not practice but a reflective theory of practice. He also suggests a point that is far from obvious: the same can be said of every branch of the study of theology. At base, Schleiermacher operated on what we today call an action-reflection model.

The action is the Christian life, the faith of the church. Being Christian, practicing Christianity, living as a Christian community in the world—these are presupposed as social facts already given in history before the study of theology is ever set up in an institution of higher learning. As soon as Christians give even a moment's thought to the life of faith, they are engaged in theology. The words and deeds of the church are its first-order theological expressions. These in turn are subject to further reflection. The result is a study of theology—probing, rigorous, critical, and constructive. To reflect in this manner one must step back, as it were, from the sheer immediacy of involvement. The step is not a retreat from faith, church, or life, but a resolve to think about the meaning of these matters with some critical distance before again jumping into action.

In the course of its historical development, the church saw fit to provide for the study of theology by giving it an institutional home in an academic setting, the university. Not every Christian could, or would, be expected to undertake this formal program of education, and those who did would not be spiritually, morally, or personally better than anyone else by virtue of having done so. But by establishing a faculty of theology and requiring a theological education for ordination, the church affirmed the desire that some of its members—those who intend to serve as its public, ordained leaders—come to their tasks with commitments informed, shaped, and tested by serious inquiry.

Wherever it is lodged and however formal it may be, the sort of theological reflection that Schleiermacher has in mind arises from the life of the Christian church. And it returns to that life. Its outcome is again a theology, this time a second-order expression of faith which, having scrutinized church practice for its Christianness, prepares for fresh engagement. Thus theology, by which Schleiermacher means Christian theology, is always church theology, and it is studied because of and for the sake of Christian practice.

If theology is church theology, and if its primary purpose is to supply the church with theologically educated leaders, does it belong alongside the sciences in an institution of higher learning? The question was hotly debated in Schleiermacher's time. He was sensitive to the issue. Early in his career he had urged Christians and "the cultured despisers of religion" to take each other more seriously; throughout his life he opposed the tendency of the learned to identify Christianity with "barbarism," and that of the faithful to associate science with "unbelief."[12] He was aware that many, both lovers and critics of Christianity, considered church theology incompatible with modern critical thinking. His own conviction was that the only theological study of genuine benefit to the church was one that met the highest standard of intellectual integrity.

Schleiermacher did not hesitate to speak of theology as a science. The term cannot be said to be easy to define with precision, then or now. Like others in the age of romanticism and idealism, Schleiermacher tried his hand at mapping out a great system of sciences that together would encompass the totality of knowledge (the ideal) about the totality of being (the real).[13] At root, however, the word "science" meant to him the pursuit of genuine knowledge through broad, deep, and critical investigation. All of the disciplines in the modern university were, or should have been, considered equally scientific in this sense. Thus he applied the term not only to those fields of study which we customarily distinguish as natural sciences, social sciences, and humanities, but also to those we call the "professional schools" of law, medicine, and theology.

Although they are equal in scientific status, these fields clearly differ in character. A key distinction, according to Schleiermacher, was that between "pure" and "positive" sciences. A pure science is one that seeks knowledge of some particular region of reality, and does so for the sake of knowledge alone. A positive science, such as law, medicine, or theology, is formed by combining various areas of inquiry—cutting across some of the pure sciences, so to speak—into a unified whole for the sake of some practical purpose. In the case of theology, the practical purpose for which various topics are combined into a field of study is the preparation of church leadership.

Schleiermacher's terminology may sound rather remote to us. The issue itself is not. Although we may be leery of the claim that any science is a "disinterested" search for knowledge for its own sake, the distinction between "pure research" and "applied research" is familiar to us. And we are well aware that the topics dealt with in seminary are highly diverse and that many, if not all, of them are, or could be, studied in any school devoted to the arts and sciences. We may learn about ancient Hebrew and Christian texts in a comparative literature course, the Renaissance and Reformation in early modern history, the ontological argument in introductory philosophy, counseling in clinical psychology, and Third-World revolutionary movements in a course on contemporary international affairs. Why, then, study or restudy, these subjects in seminary and call the outcome a "theological" education? Schleiermacher's answer is that such studies *become* theological only when they are viewed in the light of their bearing on the life of the Christian church, and, thus viewed, they prepare persons to be responsible church leaders.

By relating every branch of theology to the task of church leadership, Schleiermacher provides a goal-oriented unity to theological education. This view was hardly original with him. A theological education had long been understood as preparation for the pastorate. Schleiermacher, however, raised what had been more or less a fact of life to a matter of principle, gave it clear articulation and, by appeal to the notion of a positive science, a reasoned defense. For this reason he may be cited as the chief formulator of "the clerical paradigm" of theological education.[14]

Not every understanding and result of clerical paradigm can be traced back to Schleiermacher, however. His formal definition of the aim of theological education proved to be far more appealing than his account of that aim or his specific proposals for organizing theological study. His *Brief Outline* prompted considerable discussion, but it did not bring about the sort of radical reform he had envisioned. Commonplace in Protestantism before, during, and after Schleiermacher has been a fourfold division of the theological enterprise: Bible, church history, dogmatics (systematic theology), and practical theology. The operative assumption has been that these matters—however sliced, mixed, and supplemented—are somehow relevant to the tasks of ordained ministry. From the alternative he proposes, we can see that Schleiermacher refuses to content himself with commonplace opinions.

First, the relationship between theological study and the ministry of the church must be clarified if the unity and the value of the various theological disciplines are to be properly identified. Klaus Penzel's observation about contemporary seminary education expresses the sort of concern Schleiermacher had as well:

> Seminary students are expected to put all of their fragmented courses together and finally view them as necessary parts of an integrated whole, when, as I suspect, we ourselves, both as a faculty and individually, may all too frequently still lack such a synoptic view of

theology in which we know how to fit our own discipline and its methods as well as that of the other theological disciplines taught at our school.[15]

Obviously, we may say, the church wants seminarians to be taught any and every subject that prepares them for the demands of ministry. Unfortunately, the obviousness of it all does not produce a rationale for a coherent program of study. On the one hand, the demands of ministry are too diverse. Pressed to give their all, pastors become consummate artists in the practice of ministry. Survival demands it. Less rarely are we in a position to reflect at length about the basis and center of our ministry. Like so many artists who cannot explain the reasons for a particular combination of images on the canvas, or the way a poetic turn of phrase proves "successful," we have little control over our responses to an overload of work. We are left to wonder if our ministry has any cohesion other than our own personal energy level. In short, the demands of the parish do not automatically unify anything; on the contrary, they tend to fragment things. On the other hand, responsible church leadership surely means something other than accommodating the status quo in the church. If it did not, the only theological education that would be unified by a clerical paradigm would be one that supplied the minimum training necessary to keep the church running in place. Theory and practice would be related, but the relationship would be static and fruitless.

Second, it is necessary to resist the tendency, strong even in Schleiermacher's time, to view dogmatic or systematic theology as "theology proper," that is, the real business of theological education. When this view prevails, the other disciplines become at best mere auxiliaries to the work of the systematician. Bible and church history become so much raw material to be processed into true theology; practical studies, so many "applications" of the product. And because dogmatic or systematic theology must by necessity address basic philosophical issues, the study of theology as a whole is threatened with becoming only a steppingstone to, or a poor substitute for, serious philosophy. As such, its tie with the church seems a matter of accident or embarrassment.

Third, the status of practical theology in theological education, uncertain in the traditional schema, must be clarified and uplifted. Its relationship to the other theological disciplines as well as its own proper character require careful consideration. The term "practical theology" first appeared, it seems, in the work of the seventeenth-century theologian Gisbert Voetius. For a long time Protestants debated whether the study should focus on the practice of the Christian life or that of the ordained ministry alone. With the development of the field of Christian ethics (first conceived as "moral theology"), practical theology veered decisively in the direction of a "pastoral theology." Even so—or perhaps precisely so—its standing as a theological science came under suspicion. G.J. Planck's popular encyclopedia of 1795 relegated the field to the appendix because it dealt with the "application" rather than the "formation" of genuine knowledge.[16] Schleiermacher found previous treatments of the field to be "erratic," and often narrowly focused on preaching the Word and administering the sacraments.[17]

Schleiermacher's response to this set of issues was not merely to construct a "clerical paradigm" but to include within it a principle by which to identify the substance, the subject matter, of theological education. In this respect Schleiermacher's version of the clerical paradigm differs significantly from others before and after his time. The study of theology is not to be constructed on the basis of whatever is playing in the parish at the moment, but on a theological analysis of the *purpose* of leadership activity in the church. That purpose, according to Schleiermacher, is to insure the Christian faithfulness of the ministry of the church. Hence, whatever else church leadership seems to demand, the one thing needed is the formation of a sound understanding of the Christian religion. For this reason Christianity itself—its nature, its historical development, and its proper role in human life—must become the subject matter of theology. The study of this subject matter, Schleiermacher insisted, must be no less broad, deep, critical, and constructive than that carried on by any other science in the university. The student of theology must have a "scientific spirit" as well as a personal interest in or commitment to religion.[18]

On this basis Schleiermacher proposes a daring reorganization of the theological disciplines. Instead of the customary fourfold division comes a threefold pattern. Each is a round of inquiry with a distinct concern. Only when all three concerns have been addressed can the study of theology be said to have covered its subject matter and completed its task.

The first round of inquiry attempts to identify the defining characteristics of the faith constitutive of the Christian church. Its outcome is to be a clear conception of "the essence," the "first principles," or "Idea" of Christianity, that is, a conception of what makes the Christian religion what it truly is. Because this investigation deals with the fundamental principle(s) of the Christian religion, and since questions of principles are conceptual, philosophical matters, Schleiermacher calls this field of inquiry "philosophical theology."[19]

The second round of inquiry is the attempt to describe the condition of the faith-community in the past and the present. Its outcome will be an account of what the Christian religion has shown itself to be throughout its history. Although descriptive, the account is also evaluative and constructive. The church of the past is evaluated in light of its faithfulness to its Christian identity. And the contemporary church's understanding of faith (its *Glaubenslehre* or doctrine of faith) and morals (its *Sittenlehre* or doctrine of morals) is presented as an expression of faith appropriate to modern critical awareness. Thus biblical studies, church history, dogmatic or systematic theology (*Glaubenslehre* and *Sittenlehre*), and "church statistics"[20] are brought together under the heading "historical theology."

The third round of inquiry is practical theology. It attempts to delineate the means by which the faith-community may preserve and perfect its integrity as the present gives way to the future. Its outcome is an account of the criteria or "rules" to be used in deciding how to guide the life of the church toward the fulfillment of its Christian calling. As a "theory of practice," practical theology is not to be confused with action itself. It is the serious thinking that reviews, evaluates, and orders activities so that Christian practice never loses sight of or strays from its properly Christian aims.

To speak of these rounds of inquiry as first, second, and third is to follow what Schleiermacher calls "the most natural order" of study. It is not to rank them in order of value. Each contributes to the overall task of theological education something that the others cannot supply. Together they form an "organic unity." In the 1811 edition of the *Brief Outline* Schleiermacher drew upon the image of an organic being, a tree, in order to depict the relationship among the three disciplines. Philosophical theology is the root, historical theology the trunk, and practical theology the crown of the organism. Reference to this image was dropped from the revised edition of 1830. Schleiermacher, it seems, feared that readers would mistakenly believe that he intended to subordinate philosophical and historical theology to practical theology, when his true intention was to emphasize the equality of all three.[21]

His fear could not have been more misplaced. Criticism has almost invariably come from the opposite direction. One concern has been that the image of a tree implies that the sap, the living substance of reflection, moves from the roots through the trunk to the crown, but never in the other direction. And, indeed, despite affirming the unity, interconnection, and equality of all three disciplines, Schleiermacher himself makes a number of compromising statements. He argues that practical theology draws, and so depends, upon the interplay of philosophical and historical theology without itself exerting a direct influence on that interplay. He points out that practical theology tries to produce "rules," whereas the other fields deal in knowledge. And although in one passage he will chide those who turn practical theology into a mere "application" of dogmatics, in another passage he will speak of how the field makes use of and applies the knowledge of Christianity it receives from the other inquiries. As one commentator puts it, "while thought influences action, action does not really influence thought," and "there is a *lex credendi, lex orandi* [the rule of prayer follows the rule of faith], but no *lex orandi, lex credendi* [the rule of faith follows the rule of prayer]," and "although Schleiermacher knows, and knows thoroughly, that thought itself can be transformative, he nevertheless does not come to realize that life itself can be illuminative."[22]

The limits of Schleiermacher's view of practical theology, and those of the clerical paradigm itself, certainly deserve close scrutiny.[23] Schleiermacher typically thought of theological education in terms of partnerships—church life and academic study, religious faith and critical inquiry, and contributions from philosophical, historical, and practical theology. Whether he successfully formed those partnerships is a question for discussion. The discussion can only be helped, however, by reading Schleiermacher with care. His view of the relationship between practice (activity, life, experience) and the study of theology is multifaceted. At least three points should be kept in mind.

First, as a reflective theory of practice, practical theology makes a unique and indispensable contribution to theological education. Charles Wood has aptly summarized Schleiermacher's position:

> Leadership involves knowing *what* to do, as well as how to do it. And knowing what to do requires an understanding of the situation in which one is acting, and of the norms by which one's action is to be directed. In Schleiermacher's view, such an understanding is achieved through participation in the inquiries he called historical and philosophical theology. . . .[24]

Practical theology relies on these inquiries so that it can move on to its own proper task, which is to provide instruction about how to act. The study of theology is not complete until this third, and decisive, round of inquiry is over. The theological division of labor that Schleiermacher sketches is in no way intended to demean practical theology, much less action, the *lex orandi,* or life itself.

Second, for Schleiermacher, all theology, not just practical theology, is fundamentally reflection upon practice. It is not up to practical theology to save philosophical and historical theology from bookish abstraction. The knowledge gained from all of these inquiries is a set of judgments rooted in and accountable to the actual life-experience of the church. Indeed they are *theological* inquiries only if, and precisely because, they are related to the "fact" of Christianity. Schleiermacher adamantly denies that theology is a speculative science. Philosophical and historical theology do not deal with disembodied, timeless truths remote from "the real world" of church ministry.

Third, practical theology does have a bearing on the judgments made in philosophical and historical theology, but that bearing is indirect rather than direct. Since the results of philosophical and historical theology—a judgment about the essence of Christianity, for example—arise from an analysis of the historical life of the church, they are subject to constant revision in light of further life-experience. Inasmuch as the labors of church leaders trained in practical theology influence the church, the continuity and change which they bring about will be added, as it were, to the data base of future inquiry in philosophical and historical theology. In short, not the "findings" but the actual consequences of practical theology double back to influence work in the other two theological disciplines. Schleiermacher does not deny that "life itself can be illuminative." He holds, however, that it becomes illuminative only when one is thoughtful about it.

THE FIELD OF PRACTICAL THEOLOGY

According to Schleiermacher practical theology is developed for the sake of "maintaining and perfecting the church."[25] Those who do not care about the church can be assumed to have no need for, and hence no interest in, such a theory. Schleiermacher did not assume, however, that those who stood to benefit most from this field of theology would be convinced that a theory of practice is possible or necessary. Rely on the Holy Spirit, said some; deal with

Orientation to Schleiermacher's Practical Theology   25

each case individually, said others; personal talent makes all the difference, said yet others. The objections were many. Of what use is a theory to a practitioner?

Schleiermacher has a response in his lectures to each of these objections. His fundamental answer to the question of the possibility and necessity of a theory of practice, however, may be most readily understood by recalling the action-reflection model. People of faith are never inactive; otherwise, as Schleiermacher puts it, their faith would be dead.[26] Christian involvement in the church and the world is the action upon which a reflective theory of practical theology takes its rise. Sooner or later, one is prompted to ask, What am I doing? Why am I doing this? How should I go about doing what I should be doing? The study of theology addresses such questions in order to prepare Christians "in advance" to be intentional about their actions.

For this reason Schleiermacher claims that the study of practical theology is very much a matter of personal conscience. Everyone is active; conscientious Christians, however, are thoughtful about their activity. Realizing that their ministry may be misguided, incoherent, ineffectual, and even counterproductive, they resolve to act deliberatively. We may have hopes, for example, that our efforts will foster spiritual growth, goodwill within the congregation, or justice in the world. The gap between our hope and the reality, however, cannot be bridged unless we give second thought to our plan of action.

Giving second thought means seeking out the most appropriate way to carry out the task.[27] This instruction is precisely what practical theology is to supply. Schleiermacher calls studies dealing with "how to get something done" technical sciences or, more simply, *Technik*. Since the German term has no single English equivalent, there is merit in accepting it as a loan word. Its meaning is not difficult to explain. A technical science is an inquiry that sets out to discover which of any number of possible courses of action is best tailored to reaching a given goal. *Technik*, then, is a "theory of techniques," a set of principles, rules, or guidelines—Schleiermacher refers to "canons"—for proper action. *Technik* is of use to anyone who takes on a task that cannot be completed merely by some arbitrary or automatic action. In such cases one has to deliberate over the best way to proceed. The tasks of church leadership (*leitende Thätigkeit*, literally "guiding activity" or "activity of guidance") are just this sort, and as a "technical science," practical theology is of assistance to anyone among the clergy or laity who undertakes them.

Schleiermacher's point, which deserves special attention from twentieth-century Christians is this: Because practical theology focuses on church leadership as a whole, it cannot be merely a "pastoral theology" dealing with the work of ordained ministers alone. *Who* carries out tasks of leadership depends on the ecclesiology, the polity, and the ethos of each particular church body. Since the church expects its ordained ministers to provide guidance or leadership, pastoral responsibilities receive prominent treatment in practical theology. But the field itself is defined by the conception of guidance or leadership, not by a distinction between clergy and laity. A case could be made that neither Schleiermacher nor the church as a whole has pressed this point to full advantage.

As diverse as they are, leadership activities can be divided into two general categories: those directed toward the individuals joined in community (the local congregation) and those directed toward the community of communities (the church as a whole). Schleiermacher accordingly divides practical theology into two parts, church service (*Kirchendienst*) and church government (*Kirchenregiment*). The first, to which Schleiermacher devoted the majority of time in his lectures, deals with leadership activities within a local congregation, including worship, homiletics, "special care of souls" or pastoral care and counseling, catechetics, and missions. The overarching goal of these activities is said to be that of "nurturing the Christian disposition."[28]

The second part, church government, deals with activities relating to the larger church organization—"denominational work," as we might say today. Church government, Schleiermacher says, deals with individuals only in a derivative way. Its chief concern is to form the corporate life in such a way as to insure that Christian life will be preserved.[29] In this section questions of polity, legislation, and discipline in the church, as well as church-state relations, are addressed. The decision to include church government at all was a significant expansion of the field of practical theology, and Schleiermacher felt obliged to offer in his lectures a careful justification for it.

The technical rules that practical theology provides for these activities of church service and church government are of a special sort suited for *church* leadership. Schleiermacher emphasizes that leadership of the church is a matter of upbuilding the community and equipping the saints. It has to do with guiding, shepherding, and enabling rather than with giving orders. Harkening back to ancient Greek usage, Schleiermacher thinks of it as *psychologia*, the guidance or care of souls.³⁰ Its aim is to make a difference in the lives of people, to help them develop as they should, as individuals and as a community. For this reason, Schleiermacher suggests, we can speak of the "art of ministry" just as we speak of "the art of education" or "the art of politics." A theory of practical theology is a "theory of art" (*Kunstlehre*); its rules are "rules of art," not legalistic directives.

According to Schleiermacher, rules play a limited but crucial role in artistic endeavors. His discussion of the matter, though at times a touch demanding, is nevertheless worthy of note. Only by understanding how rules function in the art of ministry can we come to understand what practical theology can—and cannot—do to serve practitioners. On the one hand, knowing rules does not insure that artistic endeavor will be successful. Without creative vision, ability (*Talent*), and sensitivity, rules are worthless. On the other hand, unless an artist relies on rules in order to carry out a plan of action that is orderly, coherent, and appropriate to its goal, success will be unlikely and, at best, accidental. In the case of the art of ministry, Schleiermacher's message is clear. Since church leadership means dealing with people, a theory of practice is no guarantee of a "successful," that is, genuine and effective, ministry. But rules are necessary for ministerial success to be likely rather than accidental.

Deliberating among possible courses of action means to come to an informed judgment about the relationship between the condition of the church as it is and the condition of the church as it should be if it is true to its calling. Even the "thoughtless" actions of Christians—those impulsive efforts to preserve or to change the status quo, for example—betray some implicit, uncritical judgment about what the church ought to be. A reflective theory of the sort presented in practical theology makes these judgments explicit, tests whether they are appropriately Christian and maximally effective, and plans for further action. For this reason a proper concept of the church is crucial to practical theology.

By a proper concept of the church Schleiermacher means one developed by careful investigation. No views, not even those which appeal to the Bible, tradition, or philosophic wisdom, should be taken for granted. Unexamined opinions are dangerous to the church. Only searching inquiry, the interplay of historical and philosophical theology, can lead to an understanding of the church which is worthy of a truly reflective theory of practice. An understanding of this sort will be one that can identify if and when "church life" is actually in keeping with the nature and purpose of the church, indeed, with the very essence of Christianity itself. Even here, however, Schleiermacher warns against claims of infallibility. Conceptions of the church are always tentative, subject to revision in light of further experience, dialogue, and reflection.

The conception of the church which Schleiermacher uses in his own practical theology is closely related to the view of the essence of Christianity which is set forth in some of his other writings, especially in the Introduction to his dogmatics, *The Christian Faith*. His thinking on these matters is subtle, complex, and susceptible to differing interpretations. Since the topic is important if one is to understand his practical theology, a few words of explanation have to be ventured.

In the Introduction to *The Christian Faith*, Christianity is defined as "a monotheistic religion of the teleological sort in which everything is related to the redemption through Jesus Christ."[31] This definition is reached after exploring the place of religion itself within human life, the nature of religious community per se, and the distinctiveness of the Christian religious community, that is, the church. It must suffice here to lift up only a few points from the discussion.

Schleiermacher argues that religiosity emerges at the core of human selfhood, in the sphere called "immediate self-consciousness" or "feeling." Feeling—used in the singular—must not be confused with fleeting emotions prompted by one experience or another. It refers rather to the prereflective level of global self-awareness where all thinking and action have their unity. In feeling, the self is aware of itself as a center of consciousness involved in a universe of relationships with other finite beings. It is also, Schleiermacher insists, aware of its own sheer givenness. That is, the self is immediately self-conscious that its very existence amidst the totality of other finite beings is grounded upon a power *other* than itself or the finite world. Schleiermacher calls this awareness a feeling of "absolute dependence," and maintains that the word "God" first arises as the name for the "ground," the "whence," of this feeling.

With the uncovering of the feeling of absolute dependence, Schleiermacher claims to have located the defining feature of religion per se, the selfsame element at the root of every religion. But

Orientation to Schleiermacher's Practical Theology

he readily admits that to speak in this way is to deal with religion in quite abstract terms. Nowhere in human life can one point to such a thing as religion in general. There are only particular *religions,* which are communities enduring over a (long or short) period of time. In each of them the awareness of God present in feeling exhibits some particular shape and color. Schleiermacher attributes these variations among religions to the fact that the human self is a social self. On the one hand, the formation of community is a natural outgrowth of human selfhood. On the other hand, human selfhood itself is formed through interpersonal relations. Thus self-awareness, including religious self-awareness, develops in the context of a social world, and there it is always particularized.

Three elements combine to make Christianity the particular religion it is. In it the "whence" of the feeling of absolute dependence is discerned to be "the one God" beyond all finite differentiations. That is, Christianity is monotheistic. Its monotheism is distinguished from others, however, in that the awareness of relationship to God is linked to the person of Jesus Christ, who is experienced as the source which empowers members of the community to God-consciousness. Thus when Christians try to put their experience of relationship to God into words, they produce statements—the poetic language of faith with which theology begins—equating the tendency to forget God with the pain of sin, the power to attain awareness of God with the joy of grace, and identifying the one who empowers the transition from pain to joy as the Redeemer. With this experience comes an eschatological or teleological note: an impulse to realize full reconciliation between God, the self, and the world. The goal is expressed in biblical texts by the image of "the kingdom of God."

In his lectures on practical theology, Schleiermacher focuses on the particularized mode of God-consciousness within the Christian community, not on the feeling of absolute dependence in and of itself. Various terms are used to refer to it: Christian feeling, Christian piety, the Christian disposition, the common faith. The three features which combine to make this religion what it is—monotheism, teleology, redemption through Jesus Christ—are spoken of as the "Idea" of Christianity.

Like every definition, the Idea of Christianity is formal and abstract. After all, Christian churches display more than just these three elements. Schleiermacher's point, however, is that a religious community must display these three if it is in fact a Christian church. Moreover, he suggests—using language common in his day—that the Idea of Christianity is an active force that is in the process of organic development. It unfolds itself throughout history and presses toward more perfect realization in the world. Or like a "super-individual" personality, a collective consciousness, the church strives to live out, and thereby to grow into, its full identity. In sum, Schleiermacher thinks of the church found in any given time and place as a more or less pure, complete, perfect—"authentic," we might say—historical manifestation of the Idea of Christianity.

Such language will likely sound curious to readers today. Two basic points should be kept in mind, however. First, Schleiermacher is affirming that the church is and should be a redemptive community; that is its identity and its calling. Second, he is affirming that redemption is and should be experienced as a social reality. Indeed, when he speaks of the common faith of Christians, he is not simply saying that the faith of each member of the community is the same as that of every other, but that one shared faith is created through the mutual interrelationships of all. Giving and receiving—a "circulation" of religious awareness—is the life-blood of the Christian church.

What remains to be explained is how Schleiermacher fits this concept of the church into his practical theology. Obviously, the Idea of Christianity is to provide the standard by which actual conditions in the church are to be judged. Obviously, too, those judgments are to give direction to the church in its ministry. But if this standard and these judgments are to make an impact on church practice, they cannot be couched in abstract terms remote from church life as it is here and now. In the here and now there is no such thing as "Christianity in general" or "the one unified church universal." For this reason Schleiermacher could not avoid discussing the ecumenical reach, and the ecumenical limits, of his practical theology.

Because the Idea of Christianity manifests itself in the church, the Christian religion is a historical phenomenon. Schleiermacher calls it "a unity" or "a whole" that can be distinguished from other communities, secular and religious. He recognizes, however, that on this side of the kingdom, the church is a broken communion of communities. Theologians—and practical theologians in a special way—must give due regard to the specific forms in which the Idea of Christianity is to be found in the world today.

The forms, of course, are communities of faith marked by distinctively Christian piety. As such, they are to be viewed as integral parts (branches, denominations, or "parties") of the church universal. But the elements of the common faith are configured differently in these communities. Thus each of them must be said to be a more or less distinct modification of the Idea of Christianity, animated by its own particular "spirit." Of primary concern to Schleiermacher is the division between Protestantism (the Evangelical church) and Roman Catholicism. Although a reflective theory of practice must be grounded in a comprehensive (ecumenical) view of Christianity, it must also address the conditions peculiar to the community it wishes to serve. Schleiermacher therefore limits the validity of his practical theology to the confines of the Evangelical church alone.

At this point an important issue arises. If the church is a community of shared faith and if its life is a circulation of religious awareness, the very notion of church "leadership" would seem problematic. Protestantism especially has reason to be sensitive to the issue. The sixteenth-century reformers, reacting to abuses within the church's hierarchy and the gulf between clergy and laity, argued for greater equality in the church in the sense of equal access to the Word of God on the part of all Christians. Luther and Calvin, who agreed that all Christians had recourse to scripture and affirmed a "priesthood of all believers," argued nevertheless that public leaders—ordained ministers—were necessary for the church's corporate life. All Christians are priests to one another, equal before God (*coram Deo*), but the general welfare of the church as a whole requires that some be duly chosen to be its ministers. Protestantism denounced "clericalism," but acknowledged the need for an ordained ministry.

Schleiermacher, influenced significantly by the "evangelical spirit," reasoned in the same vein. He too stressed that Christians comprised a universal priesthood and that all had equal access to the Word. He also recognized that at each moment there are Christians who are "babes" in the faith and need guidance, while others are more mature and have much to offer those who are new to and weak in the faith. Some are caught in the pain of grief, and others are ready to care for them; some earnestly seek to follow the Spirit, and others are prepared to assist them in their journey. Schleiermacher based his views of church leadership on precisely these grounds. "Leaders" are those in a position to be enablers, through sermons, pastoral care, education, and the like, to assist others toward and along the path of faith.

Schleiermacher called the fact that some step forth as enablers and others are in need of their assistance "the principle of inequality" in the church. We might prefer some term other than "inequality" to speak of this distinction, but, in Schleiermacher's view, the phrase describes the situation of the church which exists in the real world of history. The need for guidance calls forth leadership activities, and leadership activities call forth a reflective theory of practice. Thus Schleiermacher says that practical theology presupposes "inequality" within the church. Opposed to clericalism, he deals at some length with the sort of inequality that practical theology presupposes. Only a few major points need to be stressed here.

From a sociological perspective, some people become enablers or leaders in the church just as some people in society become medical doctors or lawyers. Everyone in society is concerned, and has a right to be concerned, about health and about rights and obligations of citizenship. Some, however, develop their concerns to a point that they can offer others guidance about these matters. Schools of medicine and law are created to ensure that guidance will be available to the public at large. So, too, in Christianity members of the church share common concerns of faith and ministry. Some, however, accept the responsibility of offering guidance to others who wish to be equipped to share in the common task. The church establishes a formal study of theology in order to ensure that guidance will be available to the community at large.

But sociological observations need to be supplemented and corrected in light of the distinctive character of the church. Spiritually—"inwardly," as Schleiermacher sometimes says—all Christians are equal because through their faith they share a common relationship to Jesus Christ, their Redeemer. The distinction between those who emerge as leaders and the others cannot therefore be based on differences of faith.

Not all of the faithful, however, find themselves equally capable of sharing with one another the resources they have. The aptitudes and abilities of some—a way with words, for example—makes it possible for them to respond readily to the needs of others. Moreover, although all Christians share in "the common spirit" of Christianity, not all of them find themselves equally moved to express their faith through outward actions that are deliberately intended to expand the influence of the community. These differences, Schleiermacher maintains, come together and develop into a distinction between two groups in the church: those who are (relatively) more "productive," that is, capable of influencing others; and those who are (relatively) "receptive" to the influences of others. Schleiermacher's repeated references to the "relativity" of the distinction should not be missed. Receptivity does not mean inactivity; it means only that the action is expressive more of a need for strength than a power to share it. Productivity does not mean self-sufficiency; it means only that the action is expressive more of a strength to meet the needs of others than a reliance upon their help.

Finally, Schleiermacher views the distinction between the two groups in the church within its eschatological limits. By its very nature the church is "already" a community of mutual giving and receiving. But it is not yet in history a community of mutual giving and receiving in equal measure. Were the Idea of Christianity to attain perfect historical manifestation, "leadership" would be neither necessary nor possible. Schleiermacher draws from this an important conclusion: the only justification for church leadership at all is the need to move the church toward its goal of full equality. Practical theology reminds those who try to exert their influence on the church that church leadership means maintaining and perfecting the spiritual independence of every member of the community. Patterns of hierarchy, superiority and inferiority, dominance and subjugation, contradict the very nature of the church.

SPECIAL PASTORAL CARE

In speaking of faith as a living relationship with God and neighbor, Christianity has always affirmed the importance of psychological health. It has likewise always been concerned with the meaning of human fulfillment and with the path toward realizing authentic existence, "true humanity." Such terms—health, fulfillment, authenticity, true humanity—are both descriptive and normative. They refer at once to the human condition both as it is and as it should be. These are not concerns of Christians alone, of course. Every culture seeks insight into them, and develops psychological theories and practices in keeping with its insights. Christians, however, must by necessity pay heed to the theological dimensions of human selfhood, and over the centuries the ministry of the church has attended—in a wide variety of ways—to the "inner life" of the self and its course of development. According to Schleiermacher, the psychological care offered by the church should be guided by practical theology. Only by this means can it be given its proper context and proper value.

We have noted that in Schleiermacher's view the study of theology is undertaken for the sake of the church. Its purpose is to advance responsible church leadership, and responsible church leaders are to "maintain and perfect the church." Caring for the well-being of the community of faith is the primary responsibility of a Christian pastor. In some situations this responsibility can be met only by offering "care of the soul" (*Seelsorge*) to some individual member of the congregation. Schleiermacher calls this aspect of ministry "special pastoral care" or "pastoral care in the narrow sense." Today we refer to such contacts as "pastoral care relationships," and deal with them in the field of pastoral care and counseling.

The section on special pastoral care is not long, only thirty-eight pages in the German text of the *Practical Theology*. Its length, however, does not signify that Schleiermacher considered the subject uninteresting or unimportant. Merely by including it Schleiermacher gave to the infant discipline a home, and by integrating it into the very structure of practical theology he provided for it a much-needed *theological* rationale. Integrating theology and practice is very much the focus of his discussion. And it is significant that Schleiermacher, who was also a pioneer in the field of psychology, attempts the integration with considerable regard for the psychological dynamics of interpersonal relationships.

The inclusion of special pastoral care in his practical theology also indicated Schleiermacher's disagreement with the claim that ministers should not deal with the "psyche" or with personal matters. Nineteenth-century critics of pastoral care justified their stance on various grounds—a strict interpretation of the phrase "ministry of Word and Sacrament," a view of the church as a state institution, or a definition of the minister as a public teacher. Schleiermacher's defense of pastoral care grows out of his theological understanding of the church, which affirms that each individual contributes to and receives from the life of the whole. To care for the whole, a minister must care for each of its members.

The need for such care arises, Schleiermacher contends, whenever members of the congregation have come to lose their sense of identity with the faith community.[32] The loss may be due to "internal" or "external" causes, that is, to an individual's own state of mind or to the effect of some incident or situation: a personal experience such as illness or death, a sense of shame or guilt over things done, a struggle with faith or belief, disagreement with other church members or the minister, or tension and discord in a marriage or family. Whatever the cause, they no longer feel secure in their

Christian identity. They no longer contribute to or benefit from the quickening of religious awareness or the spiritual edification or the moral sensitivity of the church. They no longer mesh with the community in such a way that their needs are met or their gifts welcomed. In such cases special attention, a one-to-one relationship between the minister and the individual, is required.

Members of the church are to be bound together in genuine communion one with another, and ordained ministers of the church are mandated to nurture the sense of common identity within the church. Thus special pastoral care becomes a natural, inevitable, and valuable part of ministry. Schleiermacher even admonishes students of practical theology that "if ministers do not engage in any special care, they cannot make much of their office."[33] Making something of the office means, of course, aiding the individual in distress and thereby restoring and upbuilding the church community as a whole.

The aid, Schleiermacher insists, must be offered with prudence. It has to be tailored to actual conditions in the congregation and to the specific circumstances that occasion it. But prudent pastoral care should always be theologically informed and interpersonally sensitive. Properly combining these elements in each pastoral care relationship makes ministry an "art," and a challenging one. Perhaps the most valuable "advice" Schleiermacher gives to ministers is to remind them of the *Christian quality* of pastoral care.

The Christian quality of pastoral care, as Schleiermacher portrays it, follows from the nature of faith and the character of the religious community. Piety originates and is nourished in the communion with other Christians. Religious feeling is communicated through interpersonal relationships. *It is instrinsically relational, not individualistic.* To be a Christian community is to share, one with another, moments of religious pain and religious joy, spiritual weakness and spiritual strength, sickness and health of soul. An individual who falls out of relationship with the fellowship is a subject of concern to the community as a whole, and to the minister especially as the representative of all. Thus when he tells ministers to be aware of the condition of the community as a whole and every member in it, to take heed of public opinion, and to preserve and defend the "common feeling" present in the church, Schleiermacher is not urging them to behave like cagey politicians or mindless conformists. He is reminding them that their task is to achieve true Christian reconciliation.

Since its aim is reconciliation, pastoral care in the Protestant church which is guided by Christian quality must be in keeping with that church's "evangelical spirit." The rights and obligations of everyone in the congregation, clergy and laity alike, must be honored. These are important considerations at every point in pastoral care relationships. Indeed, the Christian quality of pastoral care begins even before a one-to-one consultation between a parishioner and a minister ever arises. It starts with the original relationship joining the congregation and its minister in life together. If that relationship is one of warmth, openness, concern, and friendliness, special pastoral care will be built on a strong foundation.

Should a minister initiate a pastoral care relationship or wait for a parishioner to request one? The question was of concern to Schleiermacher as it is to ministers today. He contrasted the situation of the Protestant church with that of Roman Catholicism, noting that due to the sacrament of Penance the Roman Catholic priest has reason to expect parishioners to seek out "the advice of clergy." No such expectation is present in Protestantism. On the contrary, by affirming the priesthood of all believers and granting each Christian direct recourse to the Bible, the Protestant church encourages each of its members to be spiritually free, independent, and self-reliant.

Spiritual freedom, however, does not mean individual isolation. Since baptism in Christ is adoption into the church as the body of Christ and since the Protestant church sets its clergy and laity in a relationship of authentic coexistence, church members should be able to trust in their ministers so that in times of need they will turn to them for help naturally. If such requests are sincere calls for aid, the minister is duty-bound to respond.

By the same token, ministers have a right to initiate a pastoral care relationship when constrained by conscience. Responsibility for the health of the community will on occasion demand direct intervention. If individuals are disturbing the common faith of the church by their behavior, for example, the minister "as the bearer and leader of public opinion," has the right to speak out and call them to account. Yet this right is not a duty. Pastors need to assess the situation and determine if intervention is likely to be productive. Only in extreme cases should they dare to act despite the likelihood of rejection. Judgments must rest on conscience and discretion, keeping in mind that the purpose of any individual relationship is to promote a stronger sense of Christian identity throughout the community.[34]

Christian identity, Christian community, Christian reconciliation—these make a pastoral care relationship a manifestation of genuine love. The solicitude of the pastor is expressive of the love within the community and, more basically, the love of God in Jesus Christ. Thus the interaction in a pastoral care relationship is that of very human concern and compassion. Stylized or manipulative behavior is altogether out of place. Love does not insist on its own way, but seeks what is best for the other. As an act of love, pastoral care should seek above all to lead the individual church member to increased spiritual maturity.

Likewise, as an act of love, pastoral care should respect the personal individuality and integrity of the church member. It must begin, proceed, and end in freedom. The spirit of the Protestant church requires that each member be granted the right to refuse to enter into personal discussions with the minister and to break them off at any time. By the same token, pastors should resist the temptation to force their own personal theological or moral views on those who come to them, lest they produce a relationship of permanent dependence or tutelage like that between a superior and a subordinate. They should instead work to restore equality by strengthening the religious resources that are already available within the individual who comes to them.

Along with love and respect, trust is essential to pastoral care relationships. Much depends, Schleiermacher believed, on the overall rapport established between the minister and the congregation. If relations are close and inviting, individual relationships will take root quite readily. If they are distant, tense, or perhaps hostile, pastoral care will be difficult to carry out. Schleiermacher points out that many factors affect this overall relationship, including what we might call sociological givens like the size of the congregation, its routinized patterns of interaction, and its constitutional order (which may be more or less explicit and easy to identify). Pastors must adapt to quite varied settings, and they must be aware that different people will perceive them differently. Schleiermacher suggests, however, that ministers are always in a position to improve the situation at least somewhat. Since pastoral care does not take place in a vacuum, often the minister's first priority has to be preparing the way for it by caring for the life of the community itself.

The trust necessary for pastoral care is also influenced by the personal attributes of the pastor. A minister who seems remote, preoccupied, biased, or harsh will discourage trust. In addition,

Schleiermacher warns against thinking that passion and zeal are the prime requisites for ministry.

> Quite generally we find that those ministers who are great zealots do not accomplish anything in pastoral care. Indeed, they accomplish less than they think they do even in public worship. But personal relationships are all but completely closed off to them.[35]

Warmth, openness, and impartiality are far more likely to elicit, and keep, the trust of those under care.

A reputation for confidentiality and discretion is also beneficial. Schleiermacher advised that although neither state nor church legislation mandated absolute confidentiality, people would not feel free to share their burdens, speak of their private affairs, or express their qualms and doubts about faith if they feared that their privacy would be violated.

In the relationship itself, ministers must be willing to suspend judgment, to express empathy, and to be flexible. If we advise, Schleiermacher cautions, then we must first be advised, in order to come to a judgment that can be mutual.[36] It is sometimes appropriate for ministers to be directive, or to speak a word of judgment. But it would not be the first word. Ministers earn the confidence of the other, and the right to speak, by first listening. Here tolerance and sympathy for the particular circumstances, motives, beliefs, and feelings of others are necessary.

Openness, however, must be combined with firm personal conviction. Pastors are not to try to be all things to all people. The attempt is futile and counterproductive. They need to be firm in their convictions, and individuals who come for counseling should be able to rely on the fact that their minister is a person of principle and integrity.

The counsel offered in a pastoral care relationship, Schleiermacher explains, should be understood by all concerned to be that of one fallible Christian to another. Though ministers must sometimes express their views candidly and firmly, they should never presume to make authoritarian statements. To do so would be to violate the Christian quality of the pastoral care relationship.

Throughout the discussion we see Schleiermacher's concern that pastors be genuine. Phoniness has no place in ministry, especially not in pastoral care where relationships are highly and subtly personal. Success in pastoral care is possible because the pastor and the parishioner share a common humanity and a common faith. But it is not inevitable. Interpersonal relationships can be fostered, aided, and guided by responsible decisions, but they neither should nor could be considered matters that pastors—or anyone else—control. Sometimes the personalities in the relationship simply do not mesh. Ministers must therefore be realistic. They should do all they can to develop the personal gifts and the "professional" skills required in pastoral care, but they will have to anticipate nonetheless that they will on occasion encounter difficulty and even failure.

To these comments about the Christian character of pastoral care relationships Schleiermacher adds words of advice about dealing with real-life situations familiar to every minister. How is a pastor to respond to those who express religious doubts or religious fanaticism? To those racked by uncertainty or guilt about their behavior? To those involved in scandals or disputes? To those contemplating divorce? To those who are terminally ill and to families who have lost a loved one? In such cases, pastors are urged to take into account personal circumstances no less than theological principles. A genuinely practical theology has something to say about the weighting of these two factors in such areas of ministry.

Of the areas he covers, two may benefit from a brief word of background. The first has to do with his views on the handling of religious doubts in a pastoral care setting. In all that he wrote, he insisted that faith is not the same as mere belief, intellectual assent, or "orthodox" opinions. It is a living relationship with God and neighbor made possible by the work of Jesus Christ and the power of the Spirit. As such, it may be true, strong, and vital even in individuals who are unable to grasp, or perhaps to go along with, formulations of doctrine developed by the church over the centuries.

For this reason Schleiermacher admonishes pastors not to lash out at parishioners who doubt or disagree with what the church, or the pastor, considers to be right belief. Calm discussion is best, and from it the pastor should gather whether the issue strikes at the heart of the person's living faith or reflects merely some confusion or quarrel about doctrinal concepts. In either case, of course, the pastor should be ready to help the parishioner understand the meaning and significance (if any) of the belief in question. But the help has to be appropriate to the parishioner's real need. Those who call upon their minister for a pastoral care relationship are not likely asking for, or served by, a crash course in systematic theology. The proper approach, Schleiermacher advises, is to draw upon and strengthen the resources that the individual already possesses.

The second area of interest is his discussion of marriage, divorce, and women's rights. Schleiermacher's views were highly progressive for the nineteenth century. He held—as his biographer Martin Redeker puts it—that

> in marriage every woman had an inalienable right to her own individuality. This romantic conception of individuality was for him in agreement with the view that a marriage in which a woman is prevented by the moral unworthiness of the other partner from developing her own individuality is no longer a marriage. . . . Therefore, he considered it his duty to dissolve such a marriage which was really no marriage.[37]

This position was not without a real-life background. While chaplain at the Charité Hospital in Berlin, Schleiermacher—then a single man around thirty years old—formed a close relationship with a woman, Eleonore Grunow, who felt trapped in an unhappy marriage. After years of waiting, he was deeply hurt when she decided that her conscience would not allow her to seek a divorce. He long remained convinced that he and Eleonore could have married and been happy. His views on the importance of nurturing the individuality of one's partner in a marriage and on insuring equal rights for a woman in marriage do not appear to have changed throughout his lifetime. Toward the end of his career, however, he argued in his Christian ethics and in some of his sermons that the indissolubility of marriage demanded that even a bad marriage be borne "penitently."[38]

The line of argument developed in his *Practical Theology* leads to the more "liberal" position that permits divorce under certain circumstances, though one can see in it how he might in later years weigh the matter differently. Throughout the discussion we see that Schleiermacher tries to deal with questions about marriage and divorce in light of theological principles *and* human realities.

In his view the theological principles themselves require careful analysis. Matthew's report that Jesus forbade divorce except in cases of adultery (Matt. 5:32)—a text often cited in the nineteenth century as well as in the twentieth—is a case in point. Schleiermacher notes that the text is clearly restrictive. But he also observes that given the laws of the times, which granted husbands arbitrary rights over their wives, the restriction on divorce in fact afforded women greater protection and equality in marriage. Not merely the words of the Bible but their historical context are taken into consideration.

On biblical and ethical grounds Schleiermacher concludes that Christianity affirms the holiness and indissolubility of marriage to be its greatest perfection. The starting point for reflection must be "the idea of the indissolubility of marriage," but—Schleiermacher adds immediately—"with the realization of course that it is only an idea."[39] When he considers the actual human experience of marriage, he concludes that in some cases a bad marriage is itself the scandal, and divorce brings the scandal to an end. Throughout his argument he recognizes that a Christian minister brings to the question concerns that the state may well overlook in its laws.

The field of pastoral care and counseling has come a long way since Schleiermacher's time, and theologically responsible Christians—as Schleiermacher himself helped teach us—cannot simply repeat what theologians of the past have said. Obviously to read his lectures on special pastoral care is not to receive the latest, or the final, word on the subject. The same must be said of his conception of practical theology itself. What we do receive, however, is perhaps of more value. We receive an invitation to reconsider for ourselves and our own time the proper relationship between theological reflection and the ministry of the church. With the invitation come issues and suggestions, from one practical theologian to another, to set us on our way.

NOTES

1. See, e.g., Matthew Lamb, "The Theory-Praxis Relationship in Contemporary Christian Theologies," in *Proceedings of the Thirty-First Annual Convention, The Catholic Theological Society of America, 1976*, ed. Luke Salm, 149–78. A helpful guide to the long philosophical discussion is Nicholas Lobkowicz, *Theory and Practice: History of a Concept from Aristotle to Marx* (Notre Dame, Ind.: Univ. of Notre Dame Press, 1967).

2. See, e.g., Don S. Browning, ed., *Practical Theology: The Emerging Field in Theology, Church, and World* (San Francisco: Harper & Row, 1983); Lewis Mudge and James Poling, eds., *Formation and Reflection: The Promise of Practical Theology* (Philadelphia: Fortress Press, 1987).

3. See the biography by Martin Redeker, *Schleiermacher: His Life and Thought*, trans. John Wallhausser (Philadelphia: Fortress Press, 1973), as well as *The Life of Schleiermacher as Unfolded in His Autobiography and Letters*, trans. Frederica Rowan, 2 vols. (London: Smith & Elder, 1860); and Brian A. Gerrish's introduction to Schleiermacher in his *A Prince of the Church: Schleiermacher and the Beginnings of Modern Theology* (Philadelphia: Fortress Press, 1984).

4. Friedrich Schleiermacher, *On Religion: Speeches to Its Cultured Des-*

pisers, trans. John Oman (London: Routledge & Kegan Paul, 1893; reprint, New York: Harper & Row, 1958); see also *On Religion: Addresses in Response to Its Cultured Despisers,* trans. and annotated by Terrence N. Tice (Richmond: John Knox Press, 1969). The *Soliloquies* have been translated by H. L. Friess (Chicago: Open Court, 1926; reprint, 1957).

5. Friedrich Schleiermacher's *Christmas Eve: A Dialogue on the Celebration of Christmas* has been twice translated: once by W. T. Hastie (Edinburgh: T. & T. Clark, 1889), and more recently by Terrence N. Tice (Richmond: John Knox Press, 1967).

6. A portion of this work is available in translation: "Reflections concerning the Nature and Function of Universities," trans. Gerhard E. Spiegler, *The Christian Scholar* 48 (1965): 139–57.

7. See also Daniel Fallon, "Friedrich Schleiermacher and the Idea of the University, Berlin, 1810–1817," in *The German University: A Heroic Ideal in Conflict with the Modern World* (Boulder: Colorado Associated Univs. Press, 1980), and Charles E. McClelland, *State, Society, and University in Germany, 1700–1914* (Cambridge: Cambridge Univ. Press, 1980).

On Schleiermacher's social and political views, and their context, see the translation of Schleiermacher's essay, "On the Concept of Different Forms of the State," in *The Political Thought of German Romantics, 1793–1815,* ed. Hans Siegbert Reiss (New York: Macmillan Co.; London: Basil Blackwell & Mott, 1955), and the (sometimes divergent) views in Robert M. Bigler, "The Rise of Political Protestantism in Nineteenth Century Germany," *Church History* 34 (1965): 423–44; idem, *The Politics of German Protestantism: The Rise of the Protestant Church Elite in Prussia, 1815–1848* (Berkeley and Los Angeles: Univ. of California Press, 1972); Richard Crouter, "Hegel and Schleiermacher in Berlin: A Many-Sided Debate," *Journal of the American Academy of Religion* 60 (1980): 285–306; Jerry F. Dawson, *Friedrich Schleiermacher: The Evolution of a Nationalist* (Austin: Univ. of Texas Press, 1966); Frederick Herzog, "Schleiermacher and the Problem of Power," *American Academy of Religion, Philosophy of Religion and Theology Proceedings, 1976,* ed. Peter Slater (Missoula, Mont.: Scholars Press, 1976), 285–99.

8. Friedrich Schleiermacher, *The Christian Faith,* trans. H. R. Mackintosh and J. S. Stewart (Edinburgh: T. & T. Clark, 1928; reprint, Philadelphia: Fortress Press, 1976).

9. Only a few sets of these lectures have been translated: *Hermeneutics: The Handwritten Manuscripts,* ed. Heinz Kimmerle, trans. James O. Duke and H. Jackson Forstman (Missoula, Mont.: Scholars Press, 1977); *The Life of Jesus,* ed. Jack C. Verheyden, trans. S. Maclean Gilmour (Philadelphia: Fortress Press, 1975).

10. Friedrich Schleiermacher, *Brief Outline on the Study of Theology,* trans. W. Farrer (Edinburgh: T. & T. Clark, 1889). A new translation has been prepared by Terrence N. Tice (Richmond: John Knox Press, 1966). Unless otherwise stated, references here will refer to the Tice translation.

11. *Die Praktische Theologie nach den Grundsätzen der evangelischen Kirche im Zusammenhange dargestellt,* in *Friedrich Schleiermachers sämmtliche Werke,* ed. Jacob Frerichs, 1.13 (Berlin: G. Reimer, 1850; reprint, Berlin: Walter De Gruyter, 1983).

Orientation to Schleiermacher's Practical Theology   43

12. In response to critics of the first edition of his dogmatics, Schleiermacher wrote an instructive commentary: *On the "Glaubenslehre": Two Letters to Dr. Lücke*, ed. and trans. James O. Duke and Francis Fiorenza (Chico, Calif.: Scholars Press, 1981), 64. On p. 61 Schleiermacher speaks of an "eternal covenant" between science and religion.

13. In this regard Wolfhart Pannenberg's discussion of the issue is valuable, *Theology and the Philosophy of Science*, trans. Francis McDonagh (Philadelphia: Westminster Press, 1973). Helpful comments on Schleiermacher's system of science can be found in Richard B. Brandt, *The Philosophy of Schleiermacher: The Development of His Theory of Science and Religious Knowledge* (New York: Harper & Brothers, 1941), chap. 6; and Gerhard Spiegler, *The Eternal Covenant: Schleiermacher's Experiment in Cultural Theology* (New York: Harper & Row, 1967).

14. The phrase is that of Edward Farley, *Theologia: The Fragmentation and Unity of Theological Education* (Philadelphia: Fortress Press, 1983), 87. Other recent treatments of Schleiermacher's *Brief Outline* include Paul D. L. Avis, "Friedrich Schleiermacher and the Science of Theology," *Scottish Journal of Theology* 32 (1979): 19–43; Karl Barth, *The Theology of Schleiermacher: Lectures at Göttingen, Winter Semester of 1923/24*, ed. Dietrich Ritschl, trans. Geoffrey W. Bromiley (Grand Rapids: Wm. B. Eerdmans, 1982), chap. 4; Brian A. Gerrish, "Continuity and Change: Friedrich Schleiermacher on the Task of Theology," in *Tradition and the Modern World: Reformed Theology in the Nineteenth Century* (Chicago: Univ. of Chicago Press, 1978), 13–48; Pannenberg, *Theology and the Philosophy of Science;* Charles Wood, *Vision and Discernment: An Orientation in Theological Study* (Atlanta: Scholars Press, 1985). Also of interest is Gerhard Ebeling, *The Study of Theology*, trans. Duane A. Priebe (Philadelphia: Fortress Press, 1978).

15. Klaus Penzel, "Some Thoughts on Schleiermacher and Practical Theology Today," *Perkins Journal* 35 (1982): 4.

16. See the historical remarks by Ebeling, *Study of Theology*, chap. 9; Farley, *Theologia*, chap. 4; Pannenberg, *Theology and the Philosophy of Science*, 429–63; Wood, *Vision and Discernment*, chap. 1.

17. See Schleiermacher, *Brief Outline*, 26, and the remarks by the translator, 125–26; cf. below, 82–83.

18. Schleiermacher, *Brief Outline*, 21–27; cf. below, 119–20.

19. See below, 96–97.

20. The *Brief Outline*, 48, states, "It is the task of Church statistics to represent the social condition of the Church at any given moment."

21. See below, 98–103.

22. John E. Burckhardt, "Schleiermacher's Vision for Theology," in *Practical Theology*, ed. Browning, 53.

23. See, e.g., comments by Farley in *Theologia*, chaps. 4 and 6, and in "Theology and Practice Outside the Clerical Paradigm," in *Practical Theology*, ed. Browning, 21–41; Pannenberg, *Theology and the Philosophy of Science*, 250–55; Penzel, "Some Thoughts on Schleiermacher and Practical Theology Today"; Wood, *Vision and Discernment*, chaps. 1 and 4.

24. Wood, *Vision and Discernment*, 12.

25. See below, 98–101. The literature in English dealing specifically with

Schleiermacher's practical theology is scarce. In addition to works already cited, one may consult Donald Groskreutz, "A Critical Study of the Thought of Friedrich Schleiermacher as Pastoral Theologian" (M.A. thesis, Univ. of Chicago, 1958); idem, "The Pastoral Theology of Friedrich Schleiermacher," *Religion in Life* 29 (1958): 557–66; Ronald Sleeth, "Schleiermacher: On Practical Theology—A Summary and an Analysis," *Princeton Seminary Bulletin* 68 (1976): 41–49.
  26. See below, 91–92.
  27. See below, 98–103.
  28. See below, 113.
  29. See below, 126.
  30. See below, 109–11.
  31. Friedrich Schleiermacher, *The Christian Faith*, par. 11 (translation our own).
  32. Cf. Schleiermacher, *Brief Outline*, 102–3.
  33. See below, 63.
  34. See below, 56.
  35. See below, 60.
  36. See below, 59–60.
  37. Redeker, *Schleiermacher*, 69–70.
  38. The phrase is that of ibid., 70; see also p. 63.
  39. See below, 75.

Translator's Note

These selections from Schleiermacher's *Praktische Theologie* have been taken from the edition prepared by Jacob Frerichs and included in Schleiermacher's *sämmtliche Werke*. The translation has been designed more for the use of seminarians, pastors, and "practical theologians" than for specialists in nineteenth-century German theology. Every translator struggles to do justice at once to both subject matter and style, for, of course, the two are finally inseparable. The struggle inevitably involves compromise, however. Whenever the need arose, I decided to compromise literal exactitude for the sake of intelligibility and readability.

A few of these decisions deserve brief comment. Throughout the text, long sentences and paragraphs have been broken up into more manageable portions, and a number of complex "if . . . then" constructions have been smoothed out into more straightforward statements. On occasion, words or short phrases necessary to make Schleiermacher's meaning explicit have been filled in. The more striking insertions have been set within brackets. Parentheses and italics follow the German text.

Perhaps more bold are the liberties taken with Schleiermacher's use of personal pronouns. The setting of the times permitted not only the use of (presumptively) gender-neutral forms of the third-person masculine singular but constant reference to ministers as males. Purist concerns notwithstanding, Schleiermacher has been permitted to speak as often as possible in sex-inclusive language. We consider the change morally sound, practically necessary, and true to the spirit of Schleiermacher's thought.

The devices used to effect this change are familiar enough and unobtrusive. Schleiermacher himself relied heavily on the German impersonal. He also sometimes switched to first-person plural forms, referring, for example, to "our church" and "our tasks." This alternative has so much to commend it that it was put to frequent use, especially in the selection on Pastoral Care.

A number of words and phrases are persistently troublesome to Schleiermacher translators. These lectures—a mixture of formal and informal discourse—contain their share of such terms. *Technik* has been left untranslated as a loan word (cf. above, 25). Where the context in German and English permits, *Bewusstsein* is translated "awareness" rather than "consciousness"; *Selbst-Bewusstsein*, "self-awareness" rather than "self-consciousness." Schleiermacher's references to *Begriff, Gedanke, Idee,* and *Vorstellung* are beholden more to ordinary language than philosophical distinctions. It nonetheless seemed advisable to indicate that Schleiermacher acknowledged the presence of a variety of more or less analytically refined terms in the language of faith and theology. Here *Begriff* becomes "concept"; *Gedanke,* "thought"; *Idee,* "Idea" (with capital I); *Vorstellung,* "idea." *Sinnliche Vorstellung* has no simple equivalent in English. It is an idea or "representation" formed as a picture of an object or state of affairs in the world of sensory perception. It is translated here as "sense-image idea." *Construieren* has a range of meanings requiring different English words—to construct, to construe, or to understand—in different contexts. The point of unity among these meanings, and the difficulty for readers unfamiliar with early nineteenth-century philosophical discourse, is the notion that things in the "real world" may be deduced, posited, or demonstrated by logical reasoning. Schleiermacher plays on these meanings when he denies that Christianity can be deduced from the principles of (absolute) Spirit or that theology, as a positive science, can be derived by deduction from "the Idea of science" alone, without reference to the life of the church.

Schleiermacher frequently attempts to identify the "individuality" of something by thinking in terms of polar opposites or "antitheses" (*Gegensätze*). That is, the particularity of an object or phenomenon is defined by noting its position between two extreme points, as we might do if we described the temperature of water coming from a faucet as a graduated mixture of hot and cold. Following this line of thought, descriptive distinctions are never absolute—tap water, for example, is said to be "hot" or "cold," but the distinction is always relative and at the mid-range shades off or

Translator's Note

"collapses." In such cases the antitheses have been translated as "extremes" or "extreme points," and the intermediary area between them, as points along a spectrum.

Topical subheadings have been inserted in the text, and two short parts of the section on Pastoral Care, dealing with responsibilities of pastors in nineteenth-century Germany with regard to counseling prisoners who await execution and administering public oaths, have been omitted. Ellipses mark where the omissions occur. The translation is otherwise a complete edition of pages 3–63 and 428–66 of the original text.

Selected Bibliography

The indispensable guide to the literature on Schleiermacher is Terrence N. Tice, *Schleiermacher Bibliography, with Brief Introductions, Annotations, and Index,* Princeton Pamphlets No. 12. Princeton: Princeton Theological Seminary, 1966. Tice has updated the work through 1984: *Schleiermacher Bibliography 1784–1984,* Princeton Pamphlets No. 101. Princeton: Princeton Theological Seminary, 1985.

Avis, Paul D. L. "Friedrich Schleiermacher and the Science of Theology." *Scottish Journal of Theology* 32 (1979): 19–43.

Barth, Karl. *Protestant Theology in the Nineteenth Century: Its Background and History.* Valley Forge, Pa: Judson Press, 1973.

———. *The Theology of Schleiermacher: Lectures at Göttingen, Winter Semester of 1923/24.* Edited by Dietrich Ritschl. Translated by Geoffrey W. Bromiley. Grand Rapids: Wm. B. Eerdmans, 1982.

Bigler, Robert M. *The Politics of German Protestantism: The Rise of the Protestant Church Elite in Prussia, 1815–1848.* Berkeley and Los Angeles: Univ. of California Press, 1972.

———. "The Rise of Political Protestantism in Nineteenth Century Germany." *Church History* 34 (1965): 423–44.

Brandt, Richard B. *The Philosophy of Schleiermacher: The Development of His Theory of Science and Religious Knowledge.* New York: Harper & Brothers, 1941.

Browning, Don S., ed. *Practical Theology: The Emerging Field in Theology, Church and World.* San Francisco: Harper & Row, 1983.

Campbell, Alastair V. "Is Practical Theology Possible?" *Scottish Journal of Theology* 25 (1972): 217–27.

———. *Rediscovering Pastoral Care.* London: Darton, Longman & Todd, 1983.

Crouter, Richard. "Hegel and Schleiermacher in Berlin: A Many-Sided Debate." *Journal of the American Academy of Religion* 60 (1980): 285–306.

Selected Bibliography

Dawson, Jerry F. *Friedrich Schleiermacher: The Evolution of a Nationalist.* Austin: Univ. of Texas Press, 1966.

———. "Friedrich Schleiermacher and the Separation of Church and State." *Journal of Church and State* 7 (1965): 214–25.

Ebeling, Gerhard. *The Study of Theology.* Translated by Duane A. Priebe. Philadelphia: Fortress Press, 1978.

Fallon, Daniel. "Friedrich Schleiermacher and the Idea of the University, Berlin, 1810–1817." In *The German University: A Heroic Ideal in Conflict with the Modern World.* Boulder: Colorado Associated Univs. Press, 1980.

Farley, Edward. "The Reform of Theological Education as a Theological Task." *Theological Education* 17 (1981): 93–117.

———. *Theologia: The Fragmentation and Unity of Theological Education.* Philadelphia: Fortress Press, 1983.

Gerrish, Brian A. *A Prince of the Church: Schleiermacher and the Beginnings of Modern Theology.* Philadelphia: Fortress Press, 1984.

———. *Tradition and the Modern World: Reformed Theology in the Nineteenth Century.* Chicago: Univ. of Chicago Press, 1978.

Greeves, Frederic. *Theology and the Cure of Souls: An Introduction to Practical Theology.* London: Epworth Press, 1960.

Grimes, Howard. "What Is Practical Theology?" *Perkins Journal* 30 (1977): 29–38.

Groskreutz, Donald. "A Critical Study of the Thought of Friedrich Schleiermacher as Pastoral Theologian." M.A. thesis, Univ. of Chicago, 1958.

———. "The Pastoral Theology of Friedrich Schleiermacher." *Religion in Life* 29 (1958): 557–66.

Herzog, Frederick. "Schleiermacher and the Problem of Power." In *American Academy of Religion, Philosophy of Religion and Theology Proceedings, 1976,* edited by Peter Slater, 285–99. Missoula, Mont.: Scholars Press, 1976.

Hiltner, Seward. *Preface of Pastoral Theology.* Nashville: Abingdon Press, 1958.

Lamb, Matthew. "The Theory-Praxis Relationship in Contemporary Christian Theologies." In *Proceedings of the Thirty-First Annual Convention, The Catholic Theological Society of America, 1976,* edited by Luke Salm, 149–78.

Lobkowicz, Nicholas. *Theory and Practice: History of a Concept from Aristotle to Marx.* Notre Dame, Ind.: Univ. of Notre Dame Press, 1967.

McClelland, Charles E. *State, Society, and University in Germany, 1700–1914.* Cambridge: Cambridge Univ. Press, 1980.

McNeill, John T. *A History of the Cure of Souls.* London: SCM Press, 1952.

Mudge, Lewis, and Poling, James, eds. *Formation and Reflection: The Promise of Practical Theology.* Philadelphia: Fortress Press, 1987.

Niebuhr, Richard R. *Schleiermacher on Christ and Religion: A New Introduction.* New York: Charles Scribner's Sons, 1964.

Oglesby, William B., Jr., ed. *The New Shape of Pastoral Theology.* Nashville: Abingdon Press, 1969.

Pannenberg, Wolfhart. *Theology and the Philosophy of Science.* Translated by Francis McDonagh. Philadelphia: Westminster Press, 1973.

Penzel, Klaus. "Some Thoughts on Schleiermacher and Pastoral Theology Today." *Perkins Journal* 35 (1982): 1–7.

Redeker, Martin. *Schleiermacher: His Life and Thought.* Translated by John Wallhausser. Philadelphia: Fortress Press, 1973.

Reiss, Hans Siegbert, ed. *The Political Thought of German Romantics, 1793–1815.* New York: Macmillan Co.; London: Basil Blackwell & Mott, 1955.

Schleiermacher, Friedrich. *Brief Outline on the Study of Theology.* Translated by Terrence N. Tice. Richmond: John Knox Press, 1966.

———. *The Christian Faith.* Translated by H.R. Mackintosh and J.S. Stewart. Edinburgh: T. & T. Clark, 1928. Reprint, Philadelphia: Fortress Press, 1976.

———. *Christmas Eve: A Dialogue on the Celebration of Christmas.* Translated by Terrence N. Tice. Richmond: John Knox Press, 1967.

———. *Hermeneutics: The Handwritten Manuscripts.* Edited by Heinz Kimmerle. Translated by James O. Duke and H. Jackson Forstman. Missoula, Mont.: Scholars Press, 1977.

———. *The Life of Jesus.* Edited by Jack C. Verheyden. Translated by S. Maclean Gilmour. Philadelphia: Fortress Press, 1975.

———. *The Life of Schleiermacher as Unfolded in His Autobiography and Letters.* Translated by Frederica Rowan. 2 vols. London: Smith & Elder, 1860.

———. *On the "Glaubenslehre": Two Letters to Dr. Lücke.* Translated by James O. Duke and Francis Fiorenza. Chico, Calif.: Scholars Press, 1981.

———. *On Religion: Addresses in Response to Its Cultured Despisers.* Translated by Terrence N. Tice. Richmond: John Knox Press, 1969.

———. *Die Praktische Theologie nach den Grundasätzen der evangelischen Kirche im Zusammenhange dargestellt.* In *Friedrich Schleiermachers sämmtliche Werke,* edited by Jacob Frerichs, vol. 1.13. Berlin: G. Reimer, 1850. Reprint, Berlin: Walter De Gruyter, 1983.

———. "Reflections concerning the Nature and Function of Universities." Translated by Gerhard E. Spiegler. *The Christian Scholar* 48 (1965): 139–57.

———. *Selected Sermons of Schleiermacher.* Translated by Mary F. Wilson. London: Hodder & Stoughton, 1890.

Sleeth, Ronald. "Schleiermacher: On Practical Theology—A Summary and an Analysis." *The Princeton Seminary Bulletin* 68 (1976): 41–49.

Spiegler, Gerhard. *The Eternal Covenant: Schleiermacher's Experiment in Cultural Theology.* New York: Harper & Row, 1967.

Stone, Howard. *Word of God and Pastoral Care.* New York: Harper & Row, 1987.

Sykes, Stephen. *Friedrich Schleiermacher.* London: Lutterworth Press, 1971; Richmond: John Knox Press, 1971.

Welch, Claude. *Protestant Thought in the Nineteenth Century.* Vol. 1. New Haven: Yale Univ. Press, 1972.

Wood, Charles. *Vision and Discernment: An Orientation in Theological Study.* Atlanta: Scholars Press, 1985.

PRACTICAL THEOLOGY:
Selections by
Friedrich Schleiermacher

Special Pastoral Care, or Pastoral Care in the Strict Sense

We now turn to that part of church service concerned with individuals who have lost their identification with the [church community as a] whole. We call this part special pastoral care or pastoral care in the strict sense of the term. We must first deal with the fact that there are those in the Evangelical church who would just as well disclaim such pastoral care, maintaining that there should not be any special relationships between ministers and members of the congregation. A minister, they say, is a public teacher, and nothing more; a minister has no right to interfere in the affairs of others and no obligation to be anything special to individuals. The rigidity of this view makes it dry and arid. It puts such distance between the minister and the congregation that authentic life together is impossible. We will see that it is obviously not correct. If someone asks to consult with us about a concern arising from our performance in the office of ministry, as ministers we simply have no right to refuse the request, and we should not try to excuse ourselves by claiming that we have to keep our distance or that we are too busy. Thus we have to grant, at least to a certain extent, that ministers are obliged to make themselves available to someone who wants to enter into a special relationship.

Yet we also have to grant something to the view that opposes special pastoral care. As ministers, we obviously have no right to interfere in the affairs of others when we are not welcome. We may have a right to try to do so under certain circumstances, but not to persist in our attempt when we are not welcome, and we are well-advised not even to try to interfere if we think we are likely to be rebuffed. But the view that opposes pastoral care relationships altogether stems from a denial of the church community itself. If the church is viewed as a political institution, serving to maintain and promote certain opinions beneficial to society under the auspices of religion, its ministers will be viewed as functionaries whose sole concern should be for their official duties.

Thus, some take as their starting point the personal freedom of every individual in the nation, and then say that although everyone must be free to use or not to use the church, which is a state institution, everyone must remain free in their own household, and that it is an intrusion when ministers interfere in family relationships. Indeed, even if the church is not viewed as an institution created by the state, so long as the task of ministry is seen to be educational, the sole responsibility of the minister will be to spare no effort in public teaching. It is always a sad view of the individual congregation—to say that there is no authentic community other than that between those who are taught and the collegium of teachers. We cannot accept this view as our point of departure. At the same time, however, the evangelical spirit of our church, in contrast to the Catholic church, places certain limits on pastoral relationships, and we must take utmost care that we not overstep them.

THE FORMATION OF PASTORAL CARE RELATIONSHIPS

We view pastoral care as a special relationship between a minister and a member of the congregation. Such a relationship will arise and develop because the minister is originally set in relationship to the congregation as a whole. A special relationship may be initiated by the minister or by some individual in the congregation. In the Catholic church the minister has a definite right to expect each member of the congregation to initiate the relationship, because each of them is obligated to make a special confession. This provides the minister the opportunity to undertake a special activity with each of them, and each of them has an obligation to submit to such activity. The right to partake of the sacrament is tied to this obligation.

Such relationships cannot be found in the Evangelical church, for we have established a different relationship between our clergy and laity, and we confer upon individual members of the congregation a status that they lack in the Catholic church. Since our church holds that each of its members has direct access to the divine Word, we allow them to direct their consciences in light of the divine Word. This difference between the two churches is so essential to the distinctive character of the Evangelical church that it must not be eliminated.

In the Evangelical church, members of the congregation cannot be obligated to establish special relationships of pastoral care. We must, therefore, ask what leads to the formation of such relationships in our church, and can we consider them to be as universal in our church as in the Catholic church? We can begin by stating that individual members of the congregation may initiate special relationships with their minister, and that they have a right to the advice of the clergy. This right can be demonstrated so conclusively that it cannot be doubted. We start with the assumption that every member of the congregation has direct access to the divine Word, can seek advice from it, and may or may not trust in their own understanding of it and in their ability to apply scriptural rules to specific situations. If a church member calls upon the minister, it is a sign that this confidence is lacking. It proves, first, that the minister's efforts to offer religious instruction and to expound the divine Word in public worship have been inadequate and have failed to fulfill their purpose. Since all of us are obliged to make up for any failure in the fulfillment of our duties, we cannot possibly refuse a member of the congregation who requests a special relationship with us. Thus the rule must be: *Whenever such requests are made, as ministers we are to use them to increase the spiritual freedom of our church members and to lead them to such clarity that no further request will be made.*

Can we, as ministers, also take the initiative in establishing a pastoral care relationship? The right to do so cannot possibly be denied us. When we speak in public, we should always speak out of our knowledge of the condition of religious awareness within the congregation as a whole; we should know what it is, and inasmuch as our speech is an act of communication, we should promote the circulation of this religious awareness so that each member of the congregation may share in the religious awareness of the whole.

We should always be aware of the condition of the congregation as a whole. But since the religious awareness of the congregation as a whole is comprised of the awareness present in each individual who belongs to the congregation, ministers must therefore be aware of public opinion with respect to the condition of each individual member. Of course, if an individual's influence on the religious awareness of the community is beneficial, the minister does not need to do anything about it. But if the influence of someone's life disturbs the religious awareness of the congregation by creating some scandal that is troubling to others or by introducing doubts in the [community's] religious awareness, the minister—as the bearer and leader of public opinion—should know about it and be affected by it, and has the right to express this opinion. Scripture itself grants this right to the minister—not to ministers as such, nor to the apostles as such, but certainly to all those who are told, "If your brother sins against you, go to him, and tell him his fault" (Matt. 18:15). Those who disturb the condition of the congregation sin against not only the congregation but its minister, because they disturb the foundation on which the minister must build. The minister therefore has the right to call them to account.

This right, however, is not a duty. As ministers we can exercise our right only if we have faith that in so doing, something will result from it. In some cases we will say, "My conscience demands that I warn this person, whether or not anything comes from it." This in no way contradicts what has just been said, for here, too, there is a faith—only it is not faith in the effect our action will have on the individual but a feeling of the need to protect ourselves and our congregation from this individual. Such a case will have to be thought of as one extreme along an infinite spectrum of finely graduated possibilities. At the other extreme are those situations when we must say, "I am simply in no position to exercise my right on this person, for he or she has withdrawn from relationship to the congregation and can be called a member of the congregation only in an external sense." A congregation is always, though only in a certain sense, an external matter—in our church [the external feature] is due to its parish connections. If persons belong to a parish and are in other respects Christians, they are members of the congregation in an external sense. If they do not take part in worship and the sacrament, they are members in the external sense alone, and they share in the community's religious awareness only externally. In this case the minister can say, "I have no right to confront these persons; such action can be taken only with those who are truly within the congregational circle."

As we operate within these extremes, we must be guided by our faith, not in the specific effect our activity may produce but only in what may result from it generally, that is, a faith that the other person will enter into relationship with us, for none of us will ever do anything that we personally consider futile. In this sense it is purely a matter of conscience how far a minister will want to go in initiating special pastoral care. We may find that even those who have been incorporated into the congregation through the public instruction they received from it may have come to a relationship with the minister of such a sort that they will not enter into a special relationship. As ministers, we are not without fault in such a situation. Our instruction should have led to a personal relationship that does not end but is continued within the congregation. Church members would then call upon us in times of need.

Now of course here, too, we come across two viewpoints. The one holds that once young people have been accepted into the congregation in an orderly way, responsibility for the salvation of their souls is transferred to them, and the bond that previously existed is dissolved. Hence, they will have to come forward themselves if they want anything from the minister. The other view, however, holds that this would be all very well and good if we could be sure that church members would always use their freedom properly. If one could view the matter purely from the standpoint of the church, one could assume that the condition of each person was fortunate. But since the matter is also entangled in social life, this certainty vanishes. For this reason it is neither advisable nor indicated by the very nature of things that the bond between the minister and the young person be considered fully dissolved.

It seems, then, that we have not been helped at all by referring back to church membership. We are, however, led to two other points. The first is that—as we have already seen—uppermost in catechetical instruction, as its true purpose, is the didactic. We should take this as our point of departure and recall what we said about carrying on catechetical instruction. The relationship formed here is one of love. If our conscience is clear about the fact that a young person has developed a personal relationship with us, we must rely on the fact that each person will turn to us. And in order to maintain good relationships, we will approach each of them—wherever we encounter them—with love. Thus a special relationship will arise naturally; by the very nature of things, each member of the congregation will turn to us, and because of this bond of love, we will be able to set to work with each of them. At the same time, all of our anxieties disappear.

The second point to which we are led is this: when young people are accepted into the congregation, they should no longer be considered isolated individuals; they have been adopted into the congregation. The individuals in the congregation cannot be viewed as set apart to themselves and as completely independent. On the contrary, each of them becomes and is part of the [community as a] whole. As ministers, we are placed in an original relationship to this whole, and of necessity there must be a relationship between the whole and the individuals in it.

The connection and ordering within a Christian congregation—whether or not they are fixed as a letter, and however they are formed—are by the very nature of things such that the minister's relationship to the [congregation as a] whole brings with it a relationship to each individual member. That is, if an individual falls into error, be it about a matter of belief or practice, which results in harm to the whole, the condition of the whole becomes unhealthy. The whole has an unhealthy member, and those who are healthy must have some means—however it may make itself manifest—to call for the care of the unhealthy member, however it may occur. Thus pastoral care becomes one of the minister's obligations toward the congregation, and there can be no talk of waiting until the individual comes to us, for we have been commissioned to act by the [congregation as a] whole. Taking this as our point of departure, we will have to say that the actual situation in the church is quite different than what it should be by the very nature of things. As ministers, we cannot decide how to proceed merely by considering the actual situation; we must also take into account what lies in the very nature of things.

If our right to initiate pastoral care must be qualified by saying that this right becomes an obligation only when there is a need to protect ourselves and our congregation from some particular individual, and if we assume that a minister will not hesitate to confront anyone about whatever seems objectionable to the congregation, then we must likewise say that in keeping with the spirit of our church, this right imposes no obligation upon the other person. It is merely an offer of a more personal relationship which everyone must remain free to accept or reject. Such a refusal can, therefore, be made in a manner proper to the church, and this is a freedom which must be permitted in the Evangelical church.

It is quite possible that although one Christian may have a clear conscience about some action or some conviction, others may take offense at it. Situations may arise, however, when individuals become convinced that it is futile to take up the matter with the minister. They must have the right to refuse an offer of a closer relationship if they think it may only create tensions with the minister. If we try to initiate a pastoral care relationship, we must do so with complete resignation, for our offer carries no authority. Since our church affirms that Christians are their own priests, such a personal relationship is nothing more than one of friendship, and it is fully a matter of freedom. This is true whether the relationship is temporary or permanent. Since we have no authority to force a member of the congregation into a relationship with us, we only weaken our authority when we often approach people with offers that are refused. Our faith in our knowledge of people is weakened, and this faith is utterly necessary for a minister. We must, therefore, proceed with great care. The more we feel an obligation to offer ourselves, the less we will need to hold back for fear of what might happen if our attempt fails. As the sense of obligation diminishes, we must give increasing attention to the possibility of failure. The decision has to be made on the basis of conscience in each individual case.

THE CONDUCT OF PASTORAL CARE

The same thing must be said about how to proceed once a pastoral care relationship has been formed. No directions can be given about what is correct. Each case is individual; universally valid directions become less significant. We can only say that the question at issue in such a relationship is whether we do more that is correct than is incorrect. There are some merely general characteristics. This much is obvious to all of us: the more there is [in our character] that hinders us, the more we show ourselves to be preoccupied when there is public opinion about a member of the congregation, the less we will be able to accomplish. The more we approach the relationship as though our judgment had been already formed, the less success we can enjoy. The more we come to it as if we wanted merely to gain more information in order to represent the congregation, the fewer obstacles we will encounter. No judgment can be made about issues that arise outside the congregation, and only these make it necessary for a minister to get involved. None of us can say that we know the motivations of another person until that person informs us about them; anything else is mere conjecture.

What a person communicates to us can be judged in different ways. A judgment about another person's relationship can be made only on the basis of deeply intimate trust. If we enter into a pastoral care relationship, we must do so only to elicit trust, so that a judgment can be given afterward. If we give advice, we must first be advised. Only by this means can we offer a judgment that can be mutual: it will be a decision made on the basis of what is actually known.

The second point is this: the more we are true to our calling to be impartial in our dealings with people of quite varied character, the more successful we will be. The more our own lives indicate that we are biased and narrow in judgment, the less competent we will be in pastoral care. People will shut themselves off from us. Therefore, quite generally we find that those ministers who are great zealots do not accomplish anything in pastoral care. Indeed, they accomplish less than they think they do even in public worship. But personal relationships are all but completely closed off to them. A zealot is always impassioned, and this passion gives people the impression of bias or limitation. When one is in a fit of passion, the receptivity that should be open is closed off, and in order to establish a relationship of trust, we must have complete emotional detachment. Everything depends on these general [personal] characteristics, which are necessary for every aspect of ministry. Related to this point is the fact that we must give due regard to the diversity of opinions and practices within the Evangelical church so that we avoid pressing the circle of what is right and good for everyone too far into specifics.

There are other personal characteristics which are less universally required. Some people elicit relationships of trust more readily than others. The more one is this sort of person, the more successful one can be in pastoral care. But there is a limit. To attempt to be such a person, or to appear as though we are, can lead to a condescending attitude that hinders the relationship and weakens our power in pastoral care. Two attitudes must be combined. We must be as receptive as possible toward different ways of acting and as mild as possible in judging them, yet at the same time we must be firm in our own judgments. If we are so empathetic with the views of others that we are determined by them and appear to be different to each person, we lose another basis for trust. People will accept a word of correction only from someone whom they regard to be of firm judgment. Without this confidence, proper trust will be missing. Trust may arise, but when it is not firm, the strength of character and the firmness of judgment of the minister who has offered himself or herself so positively come under suspicion.

Also required for the development of proper trust is the certainty that the relationship remains personal, or the assurance of confidentiality. None of us wants to reveal our innermost self without knowing to whom we are revealing it. If one cannot be sure that what is confided to someone will go no farther, there is no basis for trust. Confidentiality is ordinarily regarded as a definite obligation placed upon a minister. But there is no such obligation in the Evangelical church. The most that can be said is that as ministers we have a right to remain silent about many things that the state would not allow others to be silent about, for our relationships with members of the congregation do not exist by law but are voluntary, and personal.

Members of the congregation must be able to trust in the confidentiality of their ministers, but they cannot demand it of them; they must leave it to their ministers' judgment. This goes along with the main point, which is that through pastoral care ministers are to reconcile the individual member of the congregation with the congregation's feeling about him or her. We cannot bring about reconciliation without making use of the trust of the other person. Whether we will be satisfied with a minimum of trust [before we engage in pastoral care] is a judgment that must be left up to us as ministers. Since we must make use of the trust of the other person, we must believe that trust is present. Thus we come back to the same point: it is from the general trust between the minister and the congregation that the individual members of the congregation can develop the trust which is necessary for pastoral care and which accepts the offer for such care.

No general rules can be given, for everything depends on how the given situation relates to what is called for by the very nature of the community. If we are successful, then we were right. Of course, the question then becomes, What is the correct thing to do when we cannot be completely certain in advance? Do we dare to do what we feel led to do, or do we wait for the member of the congregation to come to us? Once again the answer depends on how great or small the danger of failure is—by which I mean not the probability, but the consequence of failure. Whenever we can rely on a truly vital relationship of community, we have it within our power to lessen the consequence of failure. If the congregation is confident that our sole concern is to advance its spiritual well-being, and if we proceed as though we were carrying out a commission from the congregation, we will always carry with us the judgment of the congregation as a whole, and thus any danger is gone. Likewise, when we go about our catechetical tasks in such a way as to create a bond of love with members of the congregation, we have already reduced the likelihood of such failure. Thus we come to the general conclusion that difficulty arises only when our bond with the congregation is not firm.

At the current time, the conditions under which ministers carry out this task of their office vary widely. At the one end of the spectrum are churches in the country; at the other end, those in big cities. In city churches the bond within the congregation is minimal. In this respect a minister can accomplish far more in small towns and in the countryside than in big cities. Thus we can identify a proper setting for each of our two contradictory rules: the rule that the minister should initiate the pastoral care relationship is more suited to close-knit congregations; the rule that members of the congregation should do so is more suited to large congregations. In some situations, of course, the reverse judgment would hold. In regions where there is no established town, where individual farms are spread out from each other, or where members of the congregation are dispersed, the bond between the individual and the congregation is weak. The relationship between the minister and each individual member of the congregation is therefore affected: we cannot be as certain of acting in the name of the community as a whole. Likewise, under a certain set of circumstances a congregation that is quite cohesive may be formed in the midst of a large city.

Those aware of what is usual and customary in the Evangelical church realize that practices vary widely. In many areas the custom is for the minister to make occasional calls upon the families and to ask how they are. In other areas this is not the case. Thus, we do not have a right to assume any one view of the relationship [between individual members of the congregation and their minister]. The relationship is not so fixed, however, that it can be demanded as one of the duties of the office. Since the relationship may be viewed more in the one way or more in the other, what is the minister to do? Since the relationship is not fixed, it can be changed. As ministers, we can adjust the relationship in one way or the other. In which way should we be inclined: to make the relationship more loose or more firm?

Once again I know of no definite decision that is to be given. But I would first want to distinguish between two cases. In the one case, we can say that the majority of the congregation is on a level equal to us with respect to spirituality; in the other, that the majority is below us. Among equals there cannot be any relationship except one of reciprocity. In this case, then, our attempts to establish a relationship with the congregation will not seem like something that must be sought for. But in the other case, we must conclude that the congregation does not want a relationship with us because it does not realize what is appropriate to its freedom. But we will also immediately say to ourselves, "If the people do not recognize my good intentions, the relationship cannot be fruitful."

In theory, we can feel free to establish pastoral care relationships whenever members of the congregation are equal to us. When they are not, we will seek to strengthen our personal authority, which will be based on the congregation's opinion of us. Therefore, in order to establish a relationship with the congregation, we have to do everything we can to gain its trust, based on respect. The invitation will then come to us from the members of the congregation themselves. If they call upon us a great deal, intervention on our part will probably be unnecessary. But if they do so only rarely, we will necessarily have to seek out such relationships, for without them our ministerial activity will not be effective. If we do not engage, and can remain without engaging, in any pastoral care relationships, we cannot possibly make much out of our office. The less often we have such relationships, the less firm our feelings will be about where a more personal relationship may or may not open up. A total lack of such relationships, however, is a sign that the condition of the congregation is less than perfect, and the problem is due, at least in part, to our own ministry. It is hard to conceive that no one is in need of personal instruction and advice. If no one calls upon us, we must awaken [the sense of] the need to do so by deliberate effort, or we must assume that the condition of the congregation is so perfect that no one requires special advice and that everything has been made clear enough [to each of them] through our public activities of ministry. But we cannot assume such a perfect condition, and the blame may fall on us as ministers for yet another reason: we do not approach members of the congregation with sufficient trust and openness, and our behavior may discourage trust. We must, therefore, seek first to establish a better relationship with the congregation as a whole.

If the sphere of religion were as separate from the sphere of the world as many think it is, it might be supposed that a minister would have difficulty gaining such a footing of trust with the congregation. But everything in life has a religious dimension and can be dealt with religiously; isolation and exclusivity of the two spheres cannot possibly persist. Once an overall relationship of trust has been established, a minister can venture into special relationships without fear of rejection. Just as in relationships of hostility neither party can ever really take any initiative, so, too, in relationships of friendship we cannot tell when the overall relationship of trust ends and a special relationship begins, or whether someone who has a special relationship with us has already made a request that went unnoticed.

Every member of a congregation has a lack and a defect for which the involvement of the minister can be of help. Yet we cannot conclude that for this reason a minister should develop a special relationship with everyone, for it is impossible for a minister to do so. Indeed, it would not be in keeping with the spirit of the Evangelical church; it would imply a tutelage such as that in the Catholic church, that is, a relationship of a confessor to a penitent. No one in our church has such a relationship either to the church or to its agents; each one should be permitted to be guided by the divine Word. We must therefore work from the assumption that no one is truly a member of the congregation except insofar as he or she has no need of spiritual tutelage. The need for such tutelage must be viewed as something existing by way of exception.

It necessarily follows that since pastoral care relationships are only temporary, they must come to a definite end. The process of pastoral care should not go on indefinitely. On the view that a pastoral care relationship arises because an individual has diverged from the congregation, we can envision two outcomes. The favorable one would be when the deviation is actually overcome. But we can also imagine the case when the change does not come about. The question then becomes whether we have a right and obligation to break off the relationship because the goal has not been reached or to continue it until the goal is reached.

By their very nature pastoral care relationships must be voluntary. They must be so from the beginning, and remain so throughout. If the minister takes the initiative, the relationship will develop only if the member of the congregation really devotes himself or herself to it, and does so from start to finish. It can be assumed that as ministers we will be willing to continue the relationship until the goal is reached. But this willingness is limited by the fact that the relationship remains free. If the freedom ends, we cannot go on with the work. Unless we become aware of some new reasons or motives to continue the process, we must concede that nothing more can be done in the present situation. There is nothing left to do but to trust that when circumstances are more favorable, when the member of

Practical Theology

the congregation has gained a clearer insight into the situation, he or she will renew the relationship.

TOPICS OF CONCERN IN PASTORAL CARE RELATIONSHIPS

We can identify two points that give rise to topics of concern in pastoral care relationships—public worship and social life. Public worship may prompt a special relationship by leading a member of the congregation to special concerns which the minister is expected to resolve. Such concerns will have to do with some question of knowledge, either knowledge about faith or about life, theory or practice. As ministers, we cannot withdraw from these concerns. Either they are the fruits of worship that we have to cultivate or they are the results of our failure to communicate the truth fully and clearly, and we have to make up for what we have failed to do.

Let us consider the other point [where concerns arise]. We realize that every aspect of social life has a religious connection and a religious value. Thus, two sorts of situations may arise. A member of the congregation may feel unable to apply general principles to specific cases. If the person comes to us, we can say, "Your knowledge will soon be corrected in public worship." But if the case is already determined by the application, then every Christian is obliged to offer advice to the other, and even more, therefore, the minister. There are also times in life when the problem is not a lack of knowledge but a feeling that one lacks the power to do what is right; in moments of temptation, for example, one may seek assistance with regard to one's moral powers. Here, too, we immediately encounter something else: one's moral powers may be so burdened that one's state of mind becomes troubled. In this case the person wants to be comforted by the minister, whereas in the first case the person wanted to be strengthened.

Do we as ministers have obligations in this situation which other Christians do not have, or are the obligations the same? If they are the same, no fixed theory can be given; the situation is covered by the rule that directs each person to use his or her gifts to aid those who are weak. Other Christians can admit that they do not know what to advise. But ministers should certainly not do this, for they would be admitting that they do not match up to the Idea of their office. Are particular skills required for such situations, and can rules be given for gaining these skills as quickly as possible at the moment? To this positive side of the question we must add a negative side: is the minister obliged to heed certain precautionary rules in these regulations?

As Protestant ministers we should assume that members of the congregation are spiritually free and independent. Yet we should seek to promote their freedom and independence as we seek to meet the demands that each of them places upon us. The rule, then, would be that *whenever such demands are made, the occasion should be used to increase the spiritual freedom of the member of the congregation and to lead him or her to such clarity that the demand will no longer arise.*

To be sure, some religious doubts are difficult to overcome, for we are dealing either with confused persons who are highly inclined toward separatism or with persons who do not really take the matter with proper seriousness and would like to embarrass us and ridicule our religious views. Confused persons cannot embarrass us; if they come to worship, their confusion will soon be resolved. On the other hand, we do not need to call separatists to account at all. We need only to reproach them for their tricks and admonish them to attend church. As soon as they do, we will address them along with everyone else. Scoffers may come to church in search of something to ridicule, or perhaps out of a love of oratory. But as ministers we are already at fault here. We have to preach such people out of the church. They should not find anything to make fun of or to perk up their ears about. We will also be able to rebuke them privately and to speak out strongly against them. Special pastoral care should always be rooted in our efforts to upbuild the congregation and to prepare for the congregation of the future, and as ministers we have no obligations in matters unrelated to these concerns.

Conviction can be communicated only by exhibiting it. It is to be assumed that as ministers we are clear about our own convictions, and we must have within ourselves everything we need to communicate them. Likewise, our calling demands that in public worship, where we are to set ourselves on the same footing with our audience, we should be familiar with the variety of opinions present in our congregation. The crucial thing is that we maintain a state of mind that enables us to communicate clearly and to take issue with those of differing views. Unless our attitude remains friendly, we will not accomplish anything.

Actually, then, only one difficulty can arise: we may find that our conviction about an issue does not seem to be one that can be communicated to the person with whom we are dealing. But here again

Practical Theology

we have to rely on the same wisdom about doctrine that we need when we lead public worship. The only difference is that in public worship we can avoid broaching topics of inquiry that cannot be communicated to the congregation, for certainly not every truth is equally good to be said in every situation, and some require that some preparation be made.

In special pastoral care we do not have this within our power. When individuals are concerned about one issue or another, we are rarely in a position to say, You should forget about this concern, for it is beyond your powers of comprehension. Ministers who use the church's creed to quash the doubts of their church members are acting like Catholics. If they repulse the doubts, or indeed if they raise the doubts themselves, they produce a result opposite to what they want. Ministers must proceed by making thoughtful decisions about the Bible and by interpreting what is obscure in light of what is clear. Of course individuals often press beyond their powers of comprehension, and in such cases the danger of suppression is greatest.

Two systems have been set up, the one designed more to bring clarity of understanding and the other more to purify [religious] feeling. These systems are derived from the distinction made in life between orthodoxy and neology. For theoretical concerns, neology is available; in order to bring peace to religious feeling, one must resort to orthodoxy. But these systems do not really work at all, for what satisfies one person's conscience does not apply at all to that of another, and what brings clarity of understanding to one person does not apply at all to another person. The neologian does not think, You will remain a neologian until your religious feelings are troubled and you will then go to your orthodox brother. Nor does the orthodox think, You will stick with the letter until it no longer satisfies you and you will then become a neologian. Neither of the two says such a thing to themselves.

If someone requires our aid in order to comfort his or her [religious] feeling, we can think of two possibilities. Either the person has never achieved a sense of inner unity and has now reached an inner crisis about attaining it, or the person has now lost the sense of life-unity which was once present. But in such a situation we should not set up a distinction between theory and dogmatics. In times when general confusion about religion prevails, the unity of religious life is easily disturbed. Thus the general question becomes, What is a minister to do to bring peace to those whose religious feeling is troubled? The main difficulty is that of bringing about a meshing of two different personalities, and the more they differ, the more the difficulty increases. The person who is the calmest, and so the strongest, will influence the one who is unsettled, and communicate peace. When the personalities are more compatible, the difficulty is eased. When they are completely incompatible, and the attitude of the one person may even repel the other, the difficulty is so significant that it often can no longer be overcome.

In such situations we must always first insist on coming to a correct idea of the importance of the issue. Clarity about the issue can be gained through an exchange of ideas. A discussion of this sort, however, requires a calm emotional state, and distress is usually due to the fact that a person overestimates the significance of the particulars of some religious idea. If requests for counsel come from members of the congregation who are accustomed to dealing with such issues, the problem will not be all that difficult [to handle]. Since they already have some knowledge of history, they can be told that there has always been uncertainty about the issue, and that this or that can be said for or against it, and that a decision is not of such great importance. But these are not the people who usually come to us for counsel, and when they do, the contact is as much a friendly one as it is an official one. For the most part, however, such questions are brought to us by the less educated members of the congregation, and we are then obliged to make up for what we should have done in our catechetical instruction.

Most questions can be traced back to several points: *the divinity of Christ, the inspiration of Scripture, the doctrine of election, and the doctrine of last things.* These give rise to most of the doubts that ministers are called upon to resolve. Although they are very different things, most can be traced back to a few points. In the case of election, the last things, and salvation, an interest in a spiritual personality is uppermost. In the case of the divinity of Christ and the inspiration of Scripture, an interest in the church is uppermost. The former interest is more subjective; the latter, more objective.

How much can be gained by first identifying the importance of the issue becomes especially evident when we consider the latter case. In dealing with doubts about inspiration, for example, we need only refer back to the early period of the church when the faith was not based on the inspiration of Scripture. And in dealing with doubts about *the divinity of Christ,* we have to call special attention to the fact that the doubt does not touch on the dignity to be ascribed to the Savior himself but only to the various ways in which Christians have appropriated this dignity in their own lives. At this point we must take special care to avoid imposing our own views on our counselees, and instead to strengthen the faith already in them and to form it religiously. A specific dogmatic formula is no support at all to such people. The doctrine of the person of Christ is in a certain sense among the topics which must be addressed through religious instruction in public worship, for the living awareness of the Savior that everyone should have must be preserved. But the formulation that this doctrine has received in the church—that is, the unity of the two natures in Christ—will never be a suitable basis for preaching. Christians are led to questions about this doctrine, however, from their readings or from their conversations with others, and thus, they may also become uncertain of their relationship to the Savior.

What must naturally be the first thing that occurs to us as ministers in this situation? Obviously, that the person may think that we should have explained the doctrine with sufficient clarity in public worship. This is the first issue that should be settled in such a situation. We should make it clear to the member of the congregation that this question has no bearing at all on the practice of Christianity itself. Once we have made this point clear, we can say, You need not be concerned because I have not spoken about this topic in public worship, and I will have to say that I cannot deal with the topic without considering it in terms of its history, and you have neither the time nor the background to go into that. We can produce the correct view of the topic only by appeal to correct immediate experience; we can cite to the member of the congregation examples of Christians who, although as devout as they were moral, nonetheless had very different views on the matter.

As for the other main topics, that is, distress about beliefs reflecting a more personal interest, how we should go to work on them depends on how the doubts arose. Unless doubts about the belief in immortality have come about because of rationalism (i.e., reflection) or they are due to the difficulty in forming a personal, definitive, sense-image of immortal life. So long as people are not troubled by such sense-image ideas, their faith does not suffer. But as soon as they are misled by the ideas that they, or others, have developed, then their conviction—which was by its very nature a sensory one—begins to waver. We must first try to steady their conviction, and to do so we must lead them to the alternative of not even trying to form a sense-image idea of immortality. They have become convinced that they cannot have firm belief because they have failed to come up with a sense-image idea of immortality and annihilation. Once we have done this, we have a common point of departure for leading them, either in a distinctively Christian or in a universally rationalistic way, to the spiritual content of the idea which cannot be grasped by means of a sense-image. Their doubt will disappear only when they become convinced that sensory certainty is impossible. We can anticipate that unless they come to this conviction, their doubt will return. *The main thing is never to lead the questioner out of the context within which the doubt arose.* We may think that people must be led into further inquiry, but by the very nature of things this suggestion will not be useful, for they lack the drive to pursue it. We must remain true to their own distinctive life-context, and seek bases of comfort there.

Doubts about divine grace are the most perplexing with which to deal. They do not depend on whether or not the topic has just been aired in the public life of the church. They usually arise from devotional readings or from contacts with people who boast of extraordinary spiritual experiences. It is especially when others have made claims about the inadequacy or necessity of such experiences that individuals are led to question whether they can be assured of their own election. The important thing here is that we become clear about the power of conflicting moments in life. If the doubt arose at the very outset of an individual's religious life, then we are faced with a different situation. But if a person who had long believed that there were good reasons for an assurance of election has suddenly become uncertain about it, then we are dealing with a conflict between different moments in life—moments of certainty and moments of uncertainty. One must then become clear about what is involved in such moments. Only then can we identify how significant the uncertainty is, and what it is based on, and we can remind our counselee that election is necessarily assured even amidst moments of great weakness. At the same time we must awaken a trust that God will not destroy what God has acted to create. Nothing depends on the letter of the doctrine or on our own understanding of it. We need only to focus on what is going on inwardly, within the soul.

Whether in such cases people can gain clarity about the issue more easily with some ministers than with others does not depend on the minister's theology but on the minister's practical competence. If the concerns arise from questions about dogmatics, the first task is to gain some distance on them. This is especially true of questions

Practical Theology

related to accounts of the doctrine of predestination which appear in one theological system or another. But since other issues are more or less similar cases, they can be handled in the same way.

An Evangelical Christian must always have free access to Scripture. Thus many issues of faith arise because people have had difficulty coming to a correct understanding of particular passages in Holy Scripture. If we, as ministers, try to present a knowledge of Scripture in such a way that conviction results, we have to enter into the field of theology, and for this reason these issues of faith are difficult to deal with. *The sin against the Holy Spirit,* for example, is a topic that has already driven many to madness. If the specter of fear has the upper hand—so much so that the people will not even turn to their minister—then no interpretation that was given in bygone days will satisfy them. Ignorance links up with obstinacy, and we are faced with the worst case of all. What is required in such cases is to be as sympathetic as possible, on the one hand, and as skillful as possible in popularizing all the results of hermeneutics, on the other. At the same time we must be concerned that even as we try to overcome one doubt, we will create another, for as we delve into Scripture, we will view other passages in a light other than that in which they are normally viewed. We will have to struggle against this evil constantly, but it is a task that we accept gladly, and we rejoice that the living spirit of our church makes it possible.

The question now becomes, *To what extent should or may we, as ministers, impose our own feelings upon members of our congregation?* When we deal with complicated cases, we must know about the various relationships involved in order to gain an overview of the whole situation. How can we gain such knowledge? This makes the giving of advice very difficult, but the difficulty is one faced not only by a minister but by every advisor. The official status of a minister modifies the situation only slightly.

The giving of advice can never be a matter of complete certainty. Either we are saying, I would act this way in this situation, or we are trying to lead the other person to clarity and to make a personal decision. The difficulty increases when background information about the situation cannot be fully disclosed without indiscretion. In such cases we must proceed very cautiously. The less we know about the situation, the more obvious it is that we are not qualified to offer any advice. To whatever we say we will have to add, The advice I give you is not based on full knowledge of the situation. It is obviously a less than perfect situation when a person who is called upon to offer a judgment about something cannot be informed of its background. We are dealing, then, with the issue of secrecy in life, and on this issue the view of the Protestant church differs from that of the Catholic church. In the Catholic church, a minister has the right to probe into even the deepest secrets, but must then observe the strictest confidentiality. In our church, however, a minister has no such right.

If someone asks us for a moral judgment, should we as ministers answer on the basis of our own feelings or on the basis of the person's feelings? Here again the two churches differ. The Catholic church does not respect the personal feelings and personal life of its individual church members as the Evangelical church does. On the contrary, the Catholic church holds that matters of uncertainty should be settled not on the basis of the individual's personal feeling but on the basis of the spirit of the church.

Those of us in the Evangelical church set out from the completely opposite view. Thus, we must ask, Is it correct or incorrect to give regard to the individual's personal feelings? No general answer can be given because the entire relationship is so transitory. An individual who has little education will have little sense of personal individuality and will be guided more by common opinion. But the stronger the individual's sense of personal individuality, the more we must take it into account and try to evaluate its validity. In such a case, we have to steady the person's feelings so that a decision may emerge by itself. In other cases, we must bring the common feeling to bear on the point of personal uncertainty. *Our own personal feeling, however, should never be the deciding factor. Either we must let the common feeling govern alone or we must free and strengthen the individual's personality.* If, as often happens, the feelings of both the minister and the member of the congregation are in conflict with the common feeling of the church to which they should be subordinate, the common feeling must take precedence. Thus, the difficulty will disappear if we have a clear idea of what we can do and what we must leave undone.

Great difficulties arise, however, when we have to be concerned about yet a third party; for example, in the case of a dispute between two people we may make a decision harmful to the other person. We must always proceed very cautiously in these situations, and we will not find it easy to do so. Here the first rule should be joined to the other. If we are successful, then we have already as good as won, for we obviously do not want to affect our relationship to the third party. But often the relationships are such that we cannot be successful. We are then in danger. We have to deal with a biased individual, and by the very nature of things we usually decide in favor of the one who turns to us. We must, therefore, guard against any biased judgments and tell the person who turns to us, Although you certainly seem to speak quite honestly, I must think about what I would have to say if the other person were here, too. We must try to protect the interest of the person who is absent, and if we do so with proper restraint, we will not harm the person who is present.

MARRIAGE COUNSELING

This leads me to an aspect of pastoral care that is official in character within the Evangelical church: *the effort to reconcile married couples who have separated.* Let us suppose that a husband or a wife brings a divorce suit before a competent judge, the complaint is accepted, and as ministers we are commissioned to attempt a reconciliation—the task is part of our job given to us by this court. There are two sides to the situation. It would have been natural for a couple that separates to have turned first to their minister. Therefore, the main point is that we should always treat each case as though it had been brought to us by the parties themselves. The situation is different if the case has been referred to us by the legal authorities, and I will deal with this instance first.

The outcome of our effort will be either favorable or unfavorable. If a reconciliation is achieved, we do not need to do anything except inform the judge that the reconciliation has been successful and that the plaintiff withdraws the suit. If the outcome is not favorable, the case proceeds through the legal process. As ministers, however, we will view the matter differently than the court. Even though the church must acknowledge the divorce, it should never desire it. The Catholic church forbids a person who has broken the marriage vow to enter into a new marriage so long as the other party is still alive. In our church the situation is as follows: Since we acknowledge the validity of a divorce granted by a judge, we should not raise any objection to a new marriage even though the former spouse is still alive. Of course, since many marriages take place only in a civil court without the minister hearing a word about it, the ecclesiastical aspect of the matter seems to have become less prominent in the Evangelical church. The difference is not equally pronounced in every case, but it seems natural for us to orient ourselves by considering the most difficult situation.

some states a marriage can be dissolved—so long as there are no children—for no other reason than that both parties favor it. Opposed to this practice is Christ's statement forbidding divorce except when the marriage is already dissolved in fact, that is, in the case of adultery (Matt. 5:32). Since as ministers we are tied to our civil office, what are we to do? Christ's statement no longer suits present-day conditions. Jewish laws granted husbands greater rights. By limiting the arbitrary acts of the husband, Christ eliminated this inequality. Viewed in this way, the word of Christ in its true sense does not conflict with today's divorce laws. We must note, however, that the holiness and indissolubility of marriage were basic to what Christ said about the topic, for in his day there was no other form of separation except this arbitrary act of a husband. Thus, we are faced with two opposing interpretations, and we cannot decide on which to put most weight—on the form current in that time or on the view which underlay it. No one will even want to make such a decision. From an ethical perspective, however, the indissolubility of marriage remains its greatest perfection; its dissolubility is merely an ethical license. Obviously, then, a minister must begin at this point.

One other form of separation is possible, however: there is a distinction between a divorce and an annulment. An annulment is permitted even by the Catholic church. It is used in the case of a marriage that should not even have existed. How is one to decide if this is the case? If we take the view that marriage is indissoluble, then every divorce is a scandal. But if the marriage should never have existed, then the marriage itself is a continuing scandal. Nothing is prescribed for us as ministers in such a case; we must therefore only satisfy our own consciences. Some may say that the only thing necessary is that we become persuaded to overturn the legal declaration. But as long as the marriage lasts, the complaint will remain, and even if the complaint is withdrawn, does the marriage become any the better? A statement of intention at the moment does no good so long as the will remains unchanged. Should we then direct our activity toward overcoming the momentary scandal of a divorce when the ongoing scandal of a bad marriage cannot be overcome? The state always distinguishes between childless couples and those with children, and it makes it more difficult to end a marriage when children are involved. The state is acting in accordance with its guardianship rights. It establishes the rule that the interest of the children

Practical Theology

demands that the marriage continue, for otherwise paternal or maternal care would cease.

What is the church's position? The church does not consider one marriage any more dissolvable than another; all marriages are equally holy. The church also sees itself as a guardian of children, for it, too, is an institution dependent on a series of generations. But its interest is exclusively religious. If the parents are granted a divorce, a very detrimental influence comes to an end. The church must, therefore, desire the divorce—assuming, of course, that the divorce itself is valid—in the interest of the children. Thus what we as ministers must defend can stand in open conflict with the intent of the law. A couple that finds itself in an unfortunate situation naturally clings to whatever promises the most satisfaction to their desires. As ministers, we receive them. Can a general rule be given for such situations? I admit that the cases are too individual for me to be able to make distinctions among the various situations that life presents. Among the lower classes the reconciliation—whatever it may be—will not be very difficult, but discord will therefore set in again all the more easily. Among the higher classes the reconciliation will be difficult, but as ministers we will also be able to rejoice all the more for having been able to achieve something. We are dealing with matters of experience and practice, but no theory can be formulated on this basis.

The task should, therefore, be approached as follows. As ministers we must start out from the Idea of the indissolubility of marriage, but with the realization of course that it is only an Idea. We must, therefore, encourage everyone to try to preserve the marriage—that is, if it is an ethical relationship, for otherwise the marriage should never have taken place. Yet we should not show any inclination, however slight, of favoring the couple's separation, unless there are quite special reasons for doing so. Even if it would have been better if the marriage had never taken place, the aggrieved party may, nevertheless, wish to endure the consequences of the marriage itself. But if special reasons are involved, the couple must separate, for the act of consummation was itself absent. Are there signs that indicate when this judgment is correct? The more we stick to the standpoint of the church, the less likely it is that anything will appear to be such a sign, and I think that the rule will always hold: There cannot be any justification for breaking up a relationship between the two persons.

In many cases even an adulterous marriage would be worthy of continuance, that is, the marriage may become better afterward than it was before. But except for this case, we do not have any right to favor the separation of a couple because of any other reason of incompatibility, not even if the marriage had taken place by force. As soon as there is a marriage, there is a principle of community. On the other hand, there can be a moral interest in allowing the separation for the sake of others, that is, the children. Thus the church's interest conflicts with that of the political authorities. From a religious viewpoint, there will often be no justification for permitting a childless couple to separate. Given this conflict, what are we to do? It is advisable to make a distinction here: the interest of the children may be served by the separation of the couple, but it may not be served by the remarriage of either parent. We will, therefore, never have any grounds for effecting a complete separation of the couple, but only a provisional reason, and it may be that the two parties will again find reason to reunite. . . .

It remains to be asked whether *ministers also need to let themselves be drawn into giving advice about matters other than those related to religion.* This frequently happens in the country [churches], and it would be wrong for ministers to avoid it, even though it is not part of pastoral care. If we assume that in most congregations the minister stands at a higher level of education [than others], we will also assume that there will naturally be an inclination to call upon the ministers for advice about various matters. As ministers, we do not have an obligation to respond to these requests, but if we understand the matter, it would be wrong for us to remain silent. Otherwise we will not be able to maintain the basis for our relationship [with the congregation].

CARE FOR THE SICK AND DYING

We now turn to discuss how to deal with those who have lost their identification with the congregation because of external circumstances, that is, care of the sick, or spiritual consolation of the sick and dying. This sort of care has been on the decrease for some time now. Whether it is a good or a bad sign is a question that can be judged in different ways. Often a great deal of superstition is mixed in with care for the sick, and if this is the reason that such care has become less frequent, there is reason to be pleased. But often it is merely the result of increasing religious indifference. I do not know what I should wish for those who hold the office of the ministry in the future: that they should engage in such care quite

Practical Theology

often or quite infrequently. For their own sakes, I would wish the former. Our wisdom about life is greatly enhanced by coming into frequent contact with those who are departing this life. But considering how the task is usually handled, I find it less joyful and uplifting. Let us begin with the worst case.

The request for a visit from the minister does not usually arrive until the time comes to administer the sacrament. There is always an element of superstition mixed in with these requests, and they are usually delayed so long that as ministers we doubt whether we can comply in good conscience. The most desirable arrangement—at least because, although extreme, it seems the only way to prevent misuse—would be for us to say that the Supper will be administered only in the church.

Even though he was about to die, Christ did not institute the Lord's Supper for his own sake, but for the sake of his disciples. Taking the Supper before death is nothing more than a superstition. We find a similar practice in the ancient church: people delayed their baptism as long as possible. This practice was due to the belief that forgiveness could not be granted, or could be granted only with great difficulty, for sins committed after baptism, and people did not wish to lapse from the state of grace. In our church the custom is to seek absolution through partaking of the Supper, and it is for this reason that people request it. In one respect the practice has something to recommend it: if someone wishes to take leave of the church, absolution will be the most perfect exhibition of this wish, and absolution occurs only in connection with the Lord's Supper. On the other hand, when the Lord's Supper is administered to an individual, the Idea of community is lost altogether, and this Idea is so essential to the act that the two can never be separated. Assuming, then, that as ministers we cannot forbid those who are ill from partaking of the Lord's Supper, I think we must insist that a community, that is, friends and family members, gather around them. *Wherever there is a community, there is a church and a congregation,* and a setting for every act of worship.

If we plan to handle the matter in this way, we will have to make our decision in advance, and linked to it must be a state of mind appropriate to the act. A correct Idea of the act can make any superstition harmless and powerless. But when our congregation does not have a constitution, we will have a hard time following through on our decision. We will have to make a rule for ourselves at the outset, and inform the congregation that only on this condition will we offer Communion to those who are ill. Assuming, then, that we have decided to make such an announcement, the question becomes whether the church government would defend and support us against opposition in the congregation, when there is no fixed constitution. *If we hold to this policy, then offering Communion to those who are ill can be of great comfort and edification to the entire family.*

Let us consider how the matter stands among the lower classes, for it hardly ever arises among the upper classes. It is a superstition to believe that an illness will turn, for life or for death, because of Communion. Often, therefore, in the case of critical illness the Lord's Supper is demanded because of the impatience of the bystanders. The sick person often knows nothing about it, and is found to be in a condition completely inappropriate for the act. Often the sick person conceals [the fact] that he or she knew nothing of the request and did not approve it. What then is the minister to do? Obviously the minister should make the situation clear. But under these circumstances nothing joyful or uplifting can be brought about, no matter what the result. The first task is always to combat the superstition. We therefore have the very difficult task of linking an action which is merely an expression of love toward the sick person with an argument against those who are healthy. The superstition must be contested on the spot.

But this is not the only superstition. Another is the belief that the sick person's salvation depends on receiving Communion—the situation is similar to the baptism of critically ill children. Once it is permitted to give Communion to those who are ill, ministers cannot go out in advance to investigate whether any superstition is present. Its presence has to be detected in the course of conversing with the sick person. The practice [of permitting those who are ill to receive Communion] is therefore very questionable. In the first example the superstition was that of the bystanders; in this case it is that of the sick person. If we begin to argue with the person, we cause distress that we cannot comfort, and we do not even know if our goal can be reached within the time remaining. We cannot even be certain if we can bring the sick person to understand how baseless their ideas are. In such a situation I cannot boast of having acted in accord with some fixed rule. If I have no hope that I can bring the person to this understanding, then I must give up the attempt and content myself with doing the opposite, that is, properly explaining the correct view. *Respect for the [person's] peace of mind during the final hours must always be the uppermost consideration.*

But there is an even worse case. When this superstition is present, the act often comes so late that it is no longer possible to come to a correct judgment about the consciousness of the sick person. Many times it is as plain as day that the sick person is no longer fully conscious. The minister then certainly has a firm right to refuse the act of Communion. Often, too, people's ideas about the sick person are incorrect. But the minister must nonetheless proceed with utmost restraint. A judgment about the situation is very doubtful because nothing can be concluded from what the sick person is saying. Either the minister cannot expect any help, or the testimony of a physician must be sought, or, if there is freedom to do so, the minister must avoid such situations, or forestall them. Ministers can probably do so in small, country congregations because they can forestall [such requests from] the family in cases of sickness. But everything depends on the relationship between the ministers and the families. The best thing to do is to adhere to the orders governing the congregation. There are few matters which intrude so much into the inner [life] of the [congregation as a] whole and which can be helped only by the orders governing the congregation than these.

THE MINISTER AND THE FUNERAL

We come now to a related matter: the activities of a minister with regard to those who have died. Some congregations require that the minister participate in every funeral. In others the minister can completely avoid the ceremony. In still others the minister is invited but given nothing to do. Our attendance in this latter situation is pointless, and we should not agree to do it. It is not proper for us, as ministers, to be merely witnesses of religious emotion without influencing it and sealing it and completing it. If we are asked to attend a funeral, we must also take an active part in it, and people need to be directed to this effect. It is not really necessary for us to ignore the funeral altogether, for it always has something religious in it, and insofar as this is so, the church community should be made aware of it. Funerals take place publicly, and church cemeteries are properties of the church. It is unnatural for the ceremony to be carried out without involving the minister as a representative of the church. In large congregations, of course, such participation is impossible. But this situation is less than perfect. As ministers we must have room to perform this natural part of our vocation.

As natural as it is for ministers to take part in the funeral service, difficulties arise even when their participation is the general practice.

As ministers we must give consideration to two elements in the ceremony: a liturgical element and a voluntary element. One tiny segment of the Protestant church has no funeral liturgy; ministers may officiate as they wish. This situation is obviously less than perfect, for there is no truly personal relationship, and a human Christian community is essential. A funeral must therefore include a liturgical element, which is inseparable from the element of the church as a whole. The liturgical element, however, is still not the same as a particular element related to the family. If we merely read the liturgy, the ceremony becomes a matter of indifference by frequent repetition. But if a voluntary religious element is added, it should be linked to the personal element, and represent the family.

Two principles come into conflict here: "speak only good of the dead," and "speak only the truth about the dead." As ministers we must be free to decide whether or not to add anything to the liturgy. Our silence in the situation certainly says enough, even though it is not definitely offensive. The situation is different when the relatives decide whether or not to demand that the minister deliver a eulogy; this practice, which is tied up with the ministerial patronage system, is a deplorable evil. There cannot be any general rules for what we should say because too much depends on the particular circumstances. As ministers we must try to soothe the pain which the relatives feel, and we will not want to say anything bitter or shameful. At the same time, we must stand before our congregation as impartial, and communicate the Word of God rightly without regard to external relationships. Our own feeling may be affected differently in different situations. The deceased may have offended many persons, and in this case especially we have to guard against giving rise to any misunderstandings, for they are right at hand. But we should not let any opportunity pass for being useful to the congregation. How things actually work out depends on the congregation's complete trust in us as its minister. . . .

With regard to the proper action to take, the only question is, Should the decision we give to a person—whether dying in a sickbed or in prison—be linked to our own dogmatic system, whatever it may be? Of course it should, if this system is so rooted in us that we think that it alone is the correct one satisfactory for Christianity. But then the farther our own viewpoint is from that of the person with whom we are dealing, the less hope we have of reaching our goal. We should not confuse theology with the essence of Christian piety, for we might then go so far as to try to restrict what is Christian to what is contained in some given system of theology. We may then come to think that we have achieved something without really having done so. We may think that we have converted the person to Christ, when he or she has actually only grasped hold of the dead letter of doctrine. But the dead letter gives no life. It is restrictive to try to connect everything back to some particular system of doctrine. Thus, what we should wish for is the facility to relate different views about one or another of the details in Christianity back to what is essential, and in holding to that. Our activity should grow out of the principle of love; the other way of acting grows out of the principle of spiritual pride and delight in a particular formulation of doctrine.

The more individual the situation and the relationships, the more difficult it is to make any general statements about them. We can say only that special attention must be given to difficult points and to the means that we apply—more to protect ourselves from such cases than to draw us into them. The congregation's view of us as ministers depends a great deal on its overall relationship with us, and, as I have already said, in many cases the only thing that can help is the influence of the congregation itself, which comes through the order present in it. But neither a minister nor the government of the church can set this order, for it must arise from the organization of the community itself.

Introduction to the Field

Practical theology is usually narrowly defined as instruction about the most appropriate way to carry out the task of teaching the divine Word and administering the sacraments. Managing the external order of Christian congregations, their ties to one another, and their relationships to civil society is said to fall outside the scope of this task. On the view that no theory can be formed about the church's relationship to society, the topic is simply omitted from the field of practical theology. I cannot agree with this view, and I have extended the boundaries of the field. We divide practical theology into two parts, *church service* and *church government*. What is frequently regarded as practical theology in its entirety is placed within the part on church service alone, and the part on church government contains much that is ordinarily excluded from practical theology.

I must first give an explanation for extending the boundaries of the field. Let us take up a general view of the Christian church as a whole, without regard to its present division [into Roman Catholicism and Protestantism]. Ever since the church came to extend over a wide territory, it has always had difficulty in determining its relationship to the state and in identifying correct principles for properly managing the order of its congregations, or even in operating as though there were such principles. Two points are at issue. First, are our ideas about these matters—given their content—suited for presentation in the form of a specific theory, and, second, is this theory in any way related to the concept of practical theology in the customary, narrow sense of the term?

Those who want to deny that a theory about these matters is necessary, or even possible, may just as well maintain that a theory

Introduction to the Field 83

about church service is superfluous. We do not find such a theory in the early ages of the Christian church, and those who became church teachers had not come from similar occupations elsewhere. Moreover, when the church expanded and it became necessary to join its various accidental elements into a coherent whole, this development took place without a theory, and yet came about as it should. As the church acquired persons of culture who had a mastery of language, and especially the language of the Holy Scripture, and since increased numbers of those who were to receive instruction from the church were unable either to appreciate or to offer judgments about art, administration came increasingly to require no more than what was asked of any person of learning. As long as one had knowledge of the Holy Scriptures, Christian doctrine, and the current state of the Christian church, as well as the general education which we presuppose as the foundation of scientific education, one did not need to preach according to a set theory. Nor was a theory required for instructing the young. Once these two tasks are removed from consideration, a theory about other matters becomes all the more superfluous. Moreover, in dealing with the doctrine of church government, one can say that although gaining the skill to know what is and is not to be done in difficult situations is certainly not easy, it depends so much on the situation and is so individual that no general theory can be developed. Thus it seems as though we need not even begin.

Let us view this subject as a matter of conscience. We develop a theory about this important task for the sake of our conscience, and the question is not how much we can accomplish by doing so, but how satisfied each of us can be with the way we carry out the task. Certainly there is such a thing as an inner perfection of the human spirit, which leads us customarily to say that people can rely completely on themselves and do not need any regulations for anything they do. Such is genius—that one is so gifted that one requires neither special training nor general rules in order to accomplish something, and yet one accomplishes it perfectly. If everyone who worked in a given field of endeavor were so gifted, no theory would be required: genius scorns rules. This is only a negative statement, however, and a positive statement must be added to it. This would be: By its excellence [of accomplishment], genius sets the rules. Thus we cannot avoid rules.

Moreover, even if such a feeling of self-reliance were sometimes required for work in some fields, the field of practical theology is not one of them. Genius is tied to the moment and is inconstant. By its very nature, however, an activity that extends beyond a single moment requires that we make some comparison between what we intend to do and a rule, if we are to be content with ourselves. Faith in the inspiration of the moment is a conceit. If it be asserted that no one would presume to do things better than the apostles, I would not try to defend myself by saying that the apostles possessed the Holy Spirit and we do not. I would certainly not like to make this claim, for the Holy Spirit is a permanent possession; otherwise, the spirit of the apostles would be of no help to us at all. Yet the object of our theory was first formed among the apostles. Someone may say that although the task of preaching was present in the patristic era, there was no theory of homiletics. Yet theory was generally available as [the discipline of] rhetoric, even though it was not applied to the church sermon because those times remained in unbroken historical continuity with antiquity, which had produced great works of eloquence. There was theory and scholastic tradition. Taste had changed, and not for the better. But theory was applied as always, and we should not let it die out.

If we set out to examine a discipline, especially one that is part of a positive science, we must first orient ourselves to its place, its conditions, and its connection with other disciplines. There are very different views on these matters within the field of theology. They are usually set forth in an encyclopedia or introduction. Practical theology especially is always treated too briefly, and given a view as narrow as the typical one, there is nothing wrong in doing so. But of course at issue here is not merely our view of practical theology but of theological science itself.

One view—which was once very widespread, later became less prominent, but now (1831) reemerges—maintains that theology proper is dogmatics, and everything else is only an auxiliary science. Since little can be said about practical theology in this respect, it is said to be "applied theology." But if theology as a whole is so defined that dogmatics becomes theology proper and practical theology merely an application of dogmatics, and if we consider how little of dogmatics—indeed nothing, insofar as it is truly dogmatics—is ever applied in the field of practical theology, then it seems to me that this view is very skewed and inadequate to the actual state of affairs.

When we ask how it has ever come about that we assemble a certain group of disciplines into what we call theology, we will have

Introduction to the Field

to identify some fixed point of departure for our inquiry. No one can possibly maintain that the science of theology—which is a positive science—can be derived from the Idea of science itself, for on that view either theological science would lose its relationship to the Christian church or the existence of the Christian church would have to be deducible from the Idea of knowledge. One of the two would have to be necessary, but neither the one nor the other is. The Christian church is a fact, and no one can deduce a fact. Nor can anyone maintain that the science of theology is not related to the Christian church. We must therefore acknowledge that the theological sciences are what they are only in relationship to the church and that they must be understood in terms of this relationship. Thus if we are to explain *how the science of theology as a whole relates to the church,* we must first come to a view of the organization of theology that is not one-sided. The account that we give of the nature and scope of practical theology can then be accepted with all the more certainty as the proper one.

Naturally we must anticipate the historical observation that this sort of inquiry does not usually arise until rather late. In this respect a positive science is quite unlike one of the pure sciences. We find that a pure science does not need to be developed very extensively before one realizes the need to ascertain its coherence in order to delimit its scope. Those dealing with a positive science find themselves in a completely different situation, for they must first ask what it is. If we want to examine the present condition of the sciences and the way they are conducted and advanced, we can do so by looking at the university. We will leave the theological faculty until last.

When we examine the study of jurisprudence, we find a mass of knowledge that is purely factual. But starting with what is factual, the study becomes scientific because of the way the knowledge is treated. Roman legislation, for example, is a pure fact; it is legislation that has emerged over time. If we ask whether the law faculty learns about this legislation solely by reference to the Roman people themselves, we will answer that this is not the point at all. What is studied is how to apply this legislation to normal cases of law. But a look at the overall organization of this field of science shows us that it includes within its purview everything considered pertinent to the administration of law in our land. Everything has been geared toward application. Since this knowledge is treated by considering not merely the letter of the law as it is set down, but how far it extends because it must be applied, members of the law faculty must identify what unifies this knowledge, and by this means the study becomes scientific in character. It remains a positive science nonetheless. Thus we clearly see that it is the character of a positive science to put together a number of elements, otherwise treated separately, by relating them to some particular practice.

Let us next examine the faculty of medicine. It deals with everything having to do with the relationship between the human organism in its conditions of health and sickness and the other powers that enter or are brought into connection with human nature, and it does so for the purpose of learning how to counteract sickness. Knowledge of nature is dealt with in a scientific manner, but it is not viewed in the same context it would be if treated from a scientific perspective. A general theory of nature cannot treat observations about the way physical bodies operate as particulars, but solely in general as universally operative powers. Medicine disregards this consideration, bringing together only those things that have a bearing on sickness and health. Matters of little scientific worth quite naturally receive as much attention as others. Everything is geared toward making the practice of medicine as good as possible. The character of this science is the same [as that of law].

Looking at the faculty of political science, we find that it too must combine elements from different sciences—politics as a philosophical discipline, but also knowledge about contemporary national affairs. The effort is to bring together whatever is needed so that those who are to lead the nation's government can do so skillfully.

What then can be said about the faculty of theology? The view which holds dogmatics to be theology proper obviously abandons this analogy with these other sciences and runs completely counter to it. If I define dogmatics as theology proper, it becomes a kind of knowledge and nothing more, although of course it is not a part of a pure science. But since dogmatics relates solely to what is Christian, this view implies that what is historical is irrelevant to Christianity. For if dogmatics is what is primary, there is no need for anything historical, and the task becomes that of convincing everyone that every dogmatic concept is a priori. Rejecting this view, we are left with only one other that corresponds fully to the analogy with the other sciences, for once we realize that all of the concepts which we thought were produced scientifically are related to particular facts, we find that we are likewise led back to what is factual.

Introduction to the Field

We should ask, though, whether dogmatics is really so much the essence of theological study that the study can be said to end with dogmatics. I would ask what one does with a dogmatic theology once one has it. When I discuss one of the pure sciences, this question never arises, for the science has its purpose in itself. I can say, I have knowledge, and I rest content with that. But if the knowledge in dogmatics is so closely bound to the fact of Christianity that the dogmatic reality of every concept is found in the realm of fact, then dogmatics is possible only in Christianity. If I then ask, what is it in Christianity? I will answer that it can be something for only a few. Since these few and everyone else in Christianity share in common something that we call faith, we will have to say that dogmatics is the highest and most perfect development, and the highest form of awareness, of this shared faith. But this awareness exists only in Christianity, and when we consider knowledge in and of itself, we must conclude that in Christianity, too, there should be an awareness of a knowledge of Christianity. Thus we are led back to the point that even in and of itself dogmatics is the perfection of the church. And if I think of the church as a moral person, dogmatics becomes the perfection of its self-awareness of its own distinctive Idea.

To desire a dogmatic theology means to desire the perfection of the Christian church. Thus dogmatics always remains related to the Christian church. Of course, no one can maintain that the perfection of the church means that some people have the perfection for themselves, while others are left with imperfection. On the contrary, no one can desire the perfection of the church without desiring a perfect contact among all of its members, without a circulation within the church itself. It is therefore improper to desire the perfection of the church only for the sake of gaining perfect knowledge of its Idea. We must instead leave the realm of pure science. No one can desire to have only one part of theology, and dogmatics is only one part related to others. All of the parts are united by their relationship to the Christian church.

This characteristic [feature] of a positive science applies to every branch of theology in the same way. For everyone will admit that what is historically related to the Christian church is no less necessary than the development of the religious idea in its perfection, because when one desires the perfection of the church, one must desire that this perfection manifest itself in history.

PRACTICAL THEOLOGY AS A THEOLOGICAL DISCIPLINE

If we then ask how practical theology fits into this [discussion], we must of course presuppose the organization of theology as a whole. The term "practical theology" itself indicates that this discipline lies closest to the practice for the sake of which the various elements of theology have been connected. We are now in a position to pursue the analogy between theology and the other sciences.

Let us begin with medicine. We note that all people to some extent care for their lives by what they take for nourishment. They bring other powers of nature into contact with the human organism, and by this means all of them come to have their own individual experiences. But this means that they are practicing medicine, and the practice is in this sense universal. If we consider nature, we find that it is always involved in the production of human life, and everything that is developed is devoted to its care. But the insights that people have, and the correctness and perfection of their insights, certainly differ greatly, and for this reason one person can be of service and use to another. If all knowledge had to be gained by personal experience, much of the knowledge that an individual gained would be useless. But physicians are those who assume leadership in human society for the care of organic processes. If all of these relationships, and society as a whole, were to lapse into such an elementary state that individuals had to care for themselves, there would be no such leadership and no medical science.

An examination of the faculties of law and political science leads us to the same conclusion. If the societies into which the human race is divided were isolated and could survive in such an elementary state, there would be no talk of a faculty of law or political science. The societies would not be able to remain in such a state for long, and after their civil elements had existed for a while, a theory would arise. What had originally consisted of an instinct undergirded by sheer force would soon be fixed in civil law by legal means, and a study of the system of law would follow. But it would be the most ridiculous thing in the world to think that such knowledge would come about because someone sat behind a desk and said, "I want to have knowledge." On the contrary, the study is always undertaken for the sake of leadership and on account of leadership. The same is true of theology. It is related to leadership of the Christian church as a society, just as these other disciplines are related to leadership of civil society and to leadership with regard to the human organism.

If we examine theology in light of this overall analogy to the idea of leadership activity, we will have little difficulty in determining the relationship between practical theology and the other theological disciplines. Strictly speaking, of course, the term "practical" is not altogether correct, for practical theology is not practice but the theory of practice. The word therefore must be taken in a figurative sense. It seems that we have now completely reversed the relationship among the disciplines. If the true goal of theology is to carry out an activity, practical theology could be said to be theology proper and the other [theological] sciences, mere auxiliaries to it. But this does not bother us, and it will become evident that the relationship among the disciplines is quite different—not one of subordination but rather more of an equality. That is, when we say that leadership activity should be carried out, we presuppose an inequality of the sort I have described when I said that the law presupposes life in society and the study of medicine presupposes an inequality with respect to the principles governing the human organism, such that a few undertake leadership activities over all. Were the Christian church to be thought of as a community of persons who, as Christians, were fully equal to each other—though in fact from the beginning such has never been the case—there never would have been any leadership activity in the church. A division of labor may certainly have developed, but it could hardly be called leadership activity.

We must now ask what produces the inequality which must be presupposed as basic to the very possibility of leadership activity. Of course I have just said that the inequality would have to go back to the origins of the church, and if so, then how it arose cannot be stated; it would seem to inhere in the essence of Christianity. But the question remains, even though the cause of the inequality lies within Christianity. One answer can be argued conclusively, but the argument leads to a result that is contrary to what actually happened. Christianity came from Christ, and was in him. Everyone else, by comparison with him, was at a null-point. There was an absolute inequality; it was at the beginning of everything that followed. Leadership activity emerged; as soon as there were believers, we see leadership activity. In this sense this inequality and this leadership activity are original to Christianity and are rooted in its essence. If the spiritual content of Christianity could have originated just as well in several people or in everyone, there would be no Christianity. There would not be a relationship to a *particular individual,* or a true object of salvation.

But if we set out from this point, we must of course say that the inequality has persisted because individuals are not equally related to Christ. The apostles were closest to him, and after he had departed, they undertook leadership activity, including a productive activity. This view of Christianity also implies, however, that we cannot assume such an inequality to continue after the apostles. The inequality between the apostles and other Christians is in no way the same as that between Christ and all other humans. The apostles themselves clearly acknowledged as much, both in their statements about their relationships to other Christians and in their actions. For by casting lots in order to complete their circle, they indicated that nothing more was required (Acts 1:26).

If we continue along this line of thinking, we are led to conclude that the inequality among Christians will decrease, and we must consider the period of leadership activity to be only a transitional stage in the life of the church. Yet even if we granted that this inner inequality were to cease completely and that in this respect everyone were equal, we would still have to acknowledge the necessity of leadership activity in the church, and we would have to look for some other source by which to account for its necessity. Christ himself clearly indicated that this inner inequality with respect to the inner power of Christianity should cease when he stated that the essence of the new covenant was that all are taught by God and no one needs to be taught by another (John 16:13; 1 John 2:27). Thus the question becomes whether there is some other inequality that always persists and necessitates an organization of the church. Here we come to a point that leads both to the true idea of theology and to the conviction that leadership activity in the church is necessary.

If we assume that there is inward equality among Christians as well as an inclination toward community which creates a corporate life so that Christianity might be communicated, and if we assume that this community encompasses the whole of Christianity, then we must also assume the possibility of a communication of all to all, for that is the conjunction of Christianity's original form and its corporate life. If we assume that everyone shared in and used the means required for such communication equally, and that everyone was in the same position, then the equality would remain perfect, and there would be no talk of any leadership activity.

But communication about religious matters—especially in Christianity, because it is expressed less in symbolic actions than in ideas and thought—is highly dependent upon the use of language. Thus this sort of perfect equality would be possible only if Christianity were limited to the use of a single language, or if there were a common language among all languages. This assumption, however, is completely unhistorical, and, obviously, can never be made. Even as we said that an inequality with regard to inner power would have to decrease, we must say that this inequality with regard to the means of religious communication will have to increase. We find that even when people share a common language, they do not have an equal mastery of it as a whole, and this inequality is linked with inequalities in education. Moreover, we must remember that Christianity did not spread all at once, and that each moment in its history must be connected with what preceded it. The language in which Christianity arose is no longer in use as a living language, and therefore each moment in its history is conditioned by the use and mastery of that language. This is one inequality that is original.

Let us now look for another point of departure. We must presuppose in the identity of faith an inclination toward community. We customarily refer to such an impulse, wherever it may be found, as the common spirit, and we always say that there cannot be any community unless there is a common spirit. But we cannot always assume that the common spirit will be distributed equally among the members of a community. On the contrary, we must assume that there is an inequality among them. This is a universal experience that we have of all communities of every sort, and the community need not even have grown very large before we observe that the common spirit is not shared equally. The form this inequality takes is that in some people the common spirit is productive, while in others it is more a living receptivity.

These two points taken together form the cardinal point that requires us to understand the Christian church as a community with an ever-recurring inequality that necessitates leadership activity. I do not think we will have any great difficulty distinguishing this sort of inequality from an inequality with respect to inner life, which must always decrease. Each of us, I think, will be immediately aware in our own self-consciousness that it is one thing to possess the spirit of Christianity inwardly and another thing to exhibit the common spirit outwardly in our actions. To be sure, those who share in the spirit of Christianity can never be inactive, or their faith would be dead. But we can understand that faith constantly gives rise to activity other than that by which the common spirit tries to influence society. The common spirit appears to be truly active in such a community, considered as an organization, and yet the impulse toward community will be distinct from the inward unification with the principle on which the community itself is founded.

We find this distinction manifest in an original way in the beginnings of Christianity. We have no reason to assume that the apostles differed among themselves with respect to their faith. To have fulfilled the role of apostle, each of them must have stood, without exception, at a distinctive level of faith: they regarded Jesus not merely as a prophet but as the one who was to come. Thus even the appearance of a significant distinction among them is dispelled. But we cannot deny that they present us with an important distinction with respect to the power of the common spirit upon them. Some stand out; others are less prominent; the activity of others has been lost to history.

At this point we can say that the Christian church presents us with a twofold principle of inequality which will always persist. There is a principle of inequality relating to the means by which the community can be maintained, and a principle of inequality relating to the influence which the Idea of the community itself has on each individual. On this basis we will have to develop our conception of what we call theological science or theological study in the context of the Christian church; that is, it is to embrace everything that allows some in the church to rise to prominence and to carry out their activities. By reference to the two principles related to this inequality, we can say that theological science embraces all of the knowledge and all of the rules of art which pertain to leadership activity in the church.

If, as I have already said, the relationship among the sciences is not to be such that the others become only auxiliaries to practical theology, we will have to say that all the rules of art relating to leadership activity belong in practical theology, while all the knowledge belongs in the other theological sciences. But this knowledge should not be viewed merely as a means to an end; it is the foundation that first makes it possible for a person, who later learns the rules of art, to carry out leadership activity that is appropriate. It is for this reason that the inequality is constantly reproduced, and we could say just as well that leadership activity is due to this recurrence of inequality as that theological science is produced. They are both the product of inequality. These major divisions—knowledge and rules of art—must therefore be set side by side as equals. We must separate them in the present context of discussion because of the way that practical theology applies this knowledge.

I must take as my point of departure the Idea at the basis of any leadership activity. Leadership activity presupposes a given condition. But to act upon this condition and to try to bring something definite from it presupposes some idea of what it is that should be brought about. Obviously we cannot think of any leadership activity unless we assume that a striving for progress accompanies it, for if nothing is to be changed, no leadership activity is required. Progress presupposes that we can envision a condition more perfect than that which is given. The question then becomes, On what basis do we arrive at this idea of a more perfect condition? But even if we restrict our attention to what is already given, our knowledge of it has to be complete and well ordered. This knowledge obviously falls into the category of historical knowledge. Thus all theological knowledge that relates in any way to our knowledge of the condition of the church is historical.

But how is one to come to this Idea of the perfect condition tnat becomes the goal toward which our leadership activity is directed? The Idea may be more or less well defined, but we must have one. The key is to identify the relationship between the given historical situation and something else to which it can be compared. If the goal of leadership activity is to make something out of the present situation, then this something is conceived as something in the future. Upon closer examination, however, we will have to say that the goal must be thought of as in some sense the final point in the future; everything else is only a transitional stage. Whether a transitional stage will be correctly identified depends on what the ultimate goal is to be, and the more directly it lies along the path leading to that goal, the better it will be identified. This goal is customarily referred to as the "ideal," that is, a state which is said to be reached by activity arising out of the present but is never reached at any given time.

Let us now ask, How are we to know if what we have thought of as the goal is correct? If we grant that some thought of its goal is required for any leadership activity, we will have to say that the concept of a historical phenomenon—which involves thinking of a series of changing conditions and comparing them—requires the ability to identify how any two given conditions differ. In order to compare a number of conditions by reference to a goal, we find it important to know whether they lie along the same path or along a deviating and partly contradictory one. At this point we will have to think of a spectrum of possibilities, for things may relate to the goal in differing ways. The one end of the spectrum represents a movement of progress; the other, a deviation which is in a certain sense a retrograde movement, for it certainly does not approach the goal as closely as it would if it had moved in a straight line.

What is the basis for such a spectrum? We could base it on something quite universal by merely saying that the one movement represents the kind that we criticize; the other, the kind that we approve. But we get nowhere this way, for we are only saying the same thing in different words. We must therefore refer again to the concept of a historical whole. Where do we encounter such a thing, and how does it originate? We note that in history [certain] activities are always linked together, and thus we must assume that there is deliberation as well as an equal stimulus coming from some given idea. If we then say that this stimulus includes a mixture of conditions that are willed and not willed, we will have a basis for a constant comparison between one thing and something else that accompanies it. We cannot designate this "something else" except by way of contrast with that which already is: it is that which ought to be, or ought to be developed. The basis for the comparison cannot be anything other than the common striving, the common impulse, viewed in two different ways.

We are not able to characterize the difference between these two ways except in general terms. Were we to suppose that such a common impulse—no matter what its object may be—were present in everyone who belonged to a historical whole and that it alone were the only thing active in them with respect to everything that belongs within the whole, we would not be able to identify anything as progress at all. The same impulse would recur, but it would not achieve anything. Any judgment about its result would be impossible. Only if the impulse changes as understanding increases over the course of time does it become possible to make a judgment. Or, if we think that it is not the impulse alone that is active but other powers at work, so that what results is due not to the impulse alone but to a combination of forces, then we will naturally identify some progress, and conclude that so long as something foreign is mixed in, the activity must be continued.

We can see, then, that the distinction between what is already given and what our activity is to bring about is based on two points: (1) that the Idea of the impulse is conceived as a thought which is in the course of development, and (2) that the impulse itself is in conflict with other powers which are active in the same domain and must be removed or brought into harmony with it. In the first instance we will characterize the condition to be judged in this way: this moment [in history] reflects a still imperfect idea of something that we wish to be perfected, something that can be reached only when the idea has attained full development. In the second instance, we will come to the judgment that this moment in history has been the result not of the impulse alone but of other powers that were active. In both cases we must say that the historical condition does not correspond to the Idea. On the one hand, the imperfect idea is not the Idea itself but a manifestation of the Idea which is thought of as still undergoing development; on the other hand, the historical condition is not composed solely of elements arising from the impulse but of something else that is mixed in. Our awareness of the true essence of the historical whole must be as perfect as possible.

For this reason, what we must set forth in our practical theology divides into two different elements. We cannot possibly come to a correct judgment about the condition of the church or point out a correct way [to progress] beyond a given condition without clear and complete knowledge of the relationship between the essence of the Christian church and its historical elements. But of course we must be modest, for even if these elements are not in and of themselves historical, they lie within the realm of history nonetheless. That is, if someone claims to have the pure concept of Christianity, someone else may say, "I doubt that; the idea you have is only a result of what has developed up to now, and only in this way have you been able to come to it; in the future a new view may emerge." No one can object to this rejoinder. The conviction is merely subjective. But this does not mean that we should give up our conviction and go over to skepticism. It means only that we must be aware of its subjectivity and be ready at every moment to begin a new inquiry so that we might enrich our view by considering the findings of others.

This leads us to another point that I have already mentioned in passing. Leadership activity presupposes inequality. I have characterized this inequality in general terms by saying that the common impulse is stronger and more complete in some people than in others—that the former are more productive; the latter, more developing. But it follows from what I have just said that this distinction between those who are prominent by virtue of their productivity and those who are receptive is only relative. What else does it mean to say that those who are productive must remain receptive to gaining information about their ideas from others? I believe that in a certain sense this is really the essential difference between the character of Protestantism and that of Catholicism. The maxims—even those that rule the church—should remain receptive to others so that a more complete view than the present one may emerge. Precisely, this is the denial of infallibility in the realm of history itself, and it is truly Protestant; whereas the claim of infallibility is the principle of Catholicism.

To return now to what is really the main point, we must say that when leadership activity is viewed from this perspective, the theological knowledge—the rules which must precede such activity—divides into two parts. The one part contains [knowledge about] what is truly historical; the other, [knowledge about] the principles of what is historical. The latter class—knowledge of principles—allows us to define the concept of the Christian church in such a way that we can evaluate and judge each moment of its history and decide which of them is better. Because this part deals with knowledge of principles, which differs in form and content from knowledge about what is actually historical, and since everything said to be a principle falls within the purview of philosophy, I have called this section of my [theological] encyclopedia "philosophical theology." In so doing, I remember that the one thing I am talking about is the principle of the Christian church, and so something which itself belongs to the church. By the same token I presuppose that the principle must encompass all of the elements that belong to the church.

There can be no talk here of principles in the speculative sense of the word, that is, principles derived from the essence of spirit, for the essence of spirit is another matter altogether than the essence of the church, and it cannot lead us to identify what is Christian. If what is Christian could be derived directly from spirit, it would have to be capable of [logical] demonstration, and one would have to disregard what is historical. But history must be presupposed. Therefore, what must be shared by all Christians—the Christian faith—should not be demonstrated from these [speculative] principles. It is to be presented in such a way that nothing emerges except the Idea of Christian faith itself, thought out in its purity and perfection. All of the other knowledge included in this field is historical, even though it depends on this Idea in a variety of ways. I first come to a historical understanding of an object in history, just as I first come to a natural understanding of an object in nature, when I know its pure concept and can determine how the condition relates to it. Without the concept, I do not have an understanding of the event, but only of its experiential elements. What turns consciousness into historical consciousness is that I know that what happened is a particular expression of its concept and that I break it down into its multiple components, some of which are especially prominent and others of which are merely coefficients.

We have already seen that the other theological disciplines should not be considered merely auxiliary to practical theology; all of the theological disciplines arise at the same time from one inner stimulus. So, too, we see that the same must be said of these two classes of knowledge. We are accustomed to thinking that principles have priority, and this is certainly correct with regard to sharing knowledge. But no such priority can be given to principles here. Although the principles are the first things at work, they are by no means the first things known, as every condition of the church, and especially its present condition, clearly shows. If people had to gain a clear awareness of principles in advance, if this action had to precede even the thought of undertaking any leadership activity, so many varied notions of the scope and essence of Christianity could not possibly have arisen. But it is likewise true that changes in the church have been of influence on the modifications of its basic ideas. Thus, like theoretical and practical theology, the two parts of theoretical theology itself—the one dealing with principles and the other dealing with what is historical—must develop at the same time.

When we reach the point when we can specify the task of practical theology, we will find it true that we must presuppose the other two branches of theology. But it is also true that we can do so only in a certain sense. We must presuppose them, for it would be foolish to try to evaluate any leadership activity without a concept of its object, and even more foolish to try to do so without having developed a clear awareness of what Christianity is, and keeping it before us. On the other hand, however, all of these [inquiries] must be interconnected, and it is here that we must contrast the principle of our church with that of the Catholic church: even in dealing with the first principles of theology we must be ready to enter into discussion with others as soon as any disagreement arises, and *no one—neither individuals, nor a group, nor even the total organi-*

zation of leaders—has a right to say that what emerges from such a discussion is false. We must therefore presuppose that two drives, which are certainly both ethical, are tightly knit together. We must immediately demand both of anyone who intends to enter the field of practical theology, [and] to take part in leadership activity. The first is that everyone will seek to bring about—given one's position in the church and one's share in its resources—what one identifies as progress. The second is that since historical investigation is necessarily required for understanding the present in light of the past, and since no judgment about the present can be considered absolutely closed, everyone must persist in research about what the limits of Christianity are and about the various forms that Christianity can take.

If we let what has been said so far stand as a preliminary reminder, we must now look over the task of practical theology as a whole in order to determine its scope and correctly divide it into its natural parts. I would like to refer to the section on practical theology in my brief theological encyclopedia. In the general introduction to that book, practical theology is defined as *the Technik for maintaining and perfecting the church* (1st ed., pars. 28–30). We can accept this definition; the immediate concern is to explain what it involves. By *Technik* we refer to instruction about how to bring something about, especially when this something is not to be brought about in a manner that is merely mechanical or completely arbitrary, for actions that are mechanical or arbitrary fall outside the scope of *Technik*. That everything we include in the meaning of the phrase "carrying out the office of ministry" should serve to *maintain* and *perfect* the Christian church—this is what is universal. Thus the definition has already pointed us to this sphere, and practical theology should show us how these tasks must be carried out in order to reach their goal. The definition itself does not mention what we have called carrying out the office of ministry; the meaning of this phrase is yet to be clarified.

This definition, however, seems to involve more than just official activities of ministry. Once the Christian church had reached a certain point of development, dogmatic theology had to emerge, and the two have been in constant interaction. The more dogmatics is perfected and refined, the more the church is perfected. We would therefore have to say that dogmatics, too, should be included in practical theology. Christian ethics, which is to direct the individual in life, could be incorporated into practical theology even more readily. Yet we never do so. The same can be said of the historical part of theology. Obviously each moment in the church's life can be rightly understood only in its historical context, and the lack of a historical view, or a false historical view, inevitably leads to confusion in the church. Thus maintaining and perfecting the Christian church would also involve disseminating historical knowledge about the church. Following this line of thinking, all of scientific theology would pass over into practical theology. Thus the question becomes, how we are to set boundaries [for the field] which are consistent with the subject matter itself.

Practical theology is the crown of theological study because it presupposes everything else; it is also the final part of the study because it prepares for direct action. Thus systematic and historical theology are presupposed by practical theology, and can in this respect be distinguished from it. But the question then becomes, By what right do we do so, and can we set the specific boundaries of the field by this means? The separation between practical theology and the other parts of scientific theology is not absolute, but merely relative. If we think of dogmatics at one stage of its development, we can presume that every improvement in it will be an improvement of the church. But dogmatics develops independently, for its own sake. Each dogmatician strives to develop the system of Christian doctrine as clearly as possible. An improvement of dogmatics in this sense, purely for its own sake, would not have anything to do with practical theology. But let us consider the matter in light of its direct bearing on the church. The development of dogmatics is not a matter of indifference, given the relationship between the state of this science and the church, although it is for the science in and of itself. Therefore practical theology enters into this area.

How then can we separate them? Neither philosophical nor historical theology is by itself included in practical theology, because although generally speaking it exists for the sake of the Christian church, taken by itself it exists even more for its own sake as a science, and not for the sake of practice in a particular church for which a *Technik* is required. Thus we do not have to limit the scope of practical theology to what is actually involved in carrying out the office of ministry. It will include every action in the church and for the church for which rules can be given.

In the special section on practical theology in my theological encyclopedia, the following definition is given: "*the task of practical theology is to bring the emotions arising in response to events in* the church into the order called for by deliberative activity" (Pt. 3, Introduction, par. 1). Let us see if this definition corresponds with that given in the Introduction. The term *Technik* presupposes that something should be done, and it is concerned with achieving this goal in a correct way. A desire to act upon the Christian church is thereby already presupposed. This desire, however, presupposes an interest. Thus practical theology exists only for the sake of those interested in bringing something about in the Christian church.

There is no such interest without an emotion. Someone wants to promote beneficial events, and unbeneficial events enter in the way. Whenever beneficial or unbeneficial events occur, they will give rise to emotions which lead to action. We presuppose here that every activity can be traced back to its origin in an emotion, and that this emotion must be known beforehand and defined as something appropriate to it. If we are indifferent to something, or if our state of mind about it is such that there is no connection with our will, we will not take any action. No action will be undertaken by a person who is indifferent to the condition of the church, or by a person who has, for example, reached a certain degree of despair. By the same token, if a person is content with the condition of the church, and thinks that it is good that things are as they are and will remain so, then once again all connection with the will is lost, since no action is considered necessary. An emotion must by necessity be presupposed, and whenever it is present, some action will result.

Practical theology is to provide directions that will make this action coherent and insure that it will not be unclear and confusing but related to a correct idea. By this means the action becomes deliberative and coherent. The aim of practical theology, therefore, is nothing other than *that of giving coherence to our activity and making it clear and deliberative*. *Technik* is the means by which an emotion is ordered into deliberative activity. Each and every technical direction suggests a way of acting tailored to its purpose. The action and its purpose are held together at each moment. In this respect these two definitions of practical theology correspond.

The second definition, however, seems to be too narrow. It presupposes that events have occurred in the church. But when one thinks of *Technik,* one presupposes only that one wishes to bring about these events. We should note, however, that even if I will to exert an influence in a given area, my activity does not follow immediately. My will must first be determined by something, which may be present in the object or in the agent. But we may be sure that the two cannot be separated. Even if an agent's will to exert an influence in a given area is more precisely determined, say, to keep in view a certain type of activity within the whole area itself, this determination does not yet lead to a certain type of activity. An external factor is required if any activity is to be undertaken. This factor may be present in the object itself, and when the object is something historical, as it is here, that factor will be an event. We can therefore conclude that a technical direction becomes an impulse only when something else spurs the interest of the individual into action. It is at this point that our second definition comes into play.

Not all emotions are unruly. This second definition, however, seems to presuppose that the emotions of those who wish to undertake activity in the church are rather unruly. We can grant that this is true of the Christian church at certain times and under certain circumstances, but not universally. But the terminology used here is less than perfect, for it is not the emotions themselves, but the action that arises from them, which should be put in order. We can therefore say that unless technical rules are provided, not even those actions arising from emotions which are not impassioned can be ordered into deliberative activity. If we are to decide on what action to take for the sake of some given goal, we need more than just emotional detachment; we also need a clear grasp of the object, the construction of the task, and the plan of operation. And this is what we mean by *Technik*. Thus the two definitions correspond.

Before proceeding farther, we have to examine more closely one other possible objection. I have stated that the goal of practical theology is to identify correctly what can be done to maintain and perfect the church. Now some have said that this is a concern to be left to God alone, that the Holy Spirit alone can produce what is correct, and that due to the distinctive character and sanctity of the object, there is no place for human art and for directions based on the idea of applying a human art. This objection must be rejected on the basis of experience, for when our action in the church takes place without regard for rules, either we produce a result contrary to that which we intended or our entire undertaking degenerates into unconscious confusion. Thus we can already see how matters stand with regard to this objection. It is correct to say that the Holy Spirit can produce only what is correct. Yet we know that none of us can boast that the Holy Spirit is the only power at work in us, and hence whatever does not proceed from the Spirit must be excluded at every moment. Moreover, no one can deny that when the Holy Spirit dwells in a person, it does so humanly, acting in a manner commensurate with human nature. Thus its effects, too, must be exhibited as something that is humanly correct. This is what we mean by art. Therefore, the activity of the Holy Spirit and art cannot come into conflict.

Some might appeal to the fact that Christ told his apostles, do not be anxious about what you should say, [for] it will be given to you by the Holy Spirit in the hour (Matt. 10:19–20), and try to make it a norm that all of the church's action must be improvised. This appeal, however, overlooks the fact that Christ was speaking of only a special case, namely, when the apostles stood before the tribunals of the pagans and had no other alternative open to them; Christ meant only to bolster their courage. This objection naturally leads us to conclude that we must come to a correct and definite idea of what rules of art can achieve, and this idea will be the same for the field of practical theology as for any other.

Let us refer back to the second definition we cited. We note that it presupposes something—an emotion must be aroused. Without an emotional arousal, no *Technik* is applied because there is no impulse for action. But this impulse is not simply directionless. If we assume that an interest in religion and Christianity is essential to everyone who is active in the field of theology, we can say that it is this interest that gives direction to all of their emotions; it leads each of them to resolve to act and makes them aware of what should be done. *Technik* serves only to specify how to go about the action.

It therefore follows that practical theology cannot establish any rules that are productive; that is, its rules do not make anyone an agent or call forth any action. But once a person decides to act, the rules guide the person in carrying out the action correctly. This is true in every field of endeavor. Detailed knowledge about musical composition does not make anyone a composer. Rules cannot produce creativity. But once a creative impulse arises in the soul, rules serve to guide how to go about the work. Thus we see that there is no conflict between acknowledging the activity of the Holy Spirit throughout the church and making use of art. We must rely on the Holy Spirit to produce the impulse and the original resolve to take correct action, but the external performance of the action will be all the more perfect when it is human and accords with rules for human arts. The impulse and the factor of genius are due to the Holy Spirit; *Technik* applies to the activity itself, which is to be in the service of that impulse and receives its inner determination from it. Nothing in Scripture, nor in experience—even our experience of action in the church, if we judge by results—indicates that the activity of the Holy Spirit can substitute for scientific effort and art. The divine principle in the Christian congregation is a spirit of order; barbarism, however, can never be ordered. To dispense with this guiding principle would be to contradict the true reality of the Holy Spirit.

This discussion has allowed us to determine the precise value of practical theology as *Technik*. We can therefore add something else in order to reassure those who may be inclined to give credence to this objection. *Technik* is used in this context to specify the correct way to carry out a task that is already given. Therefore, nothing should be set up as a rule that may in any way endanger, or oppose, the continuation and perfection of the Christian church. Thus we prevent any possible misuse (of rules). Both of our definitions are based on the Idea of art. Of course, degeneracy can be found in every human art. Before the art has reached a certain point of development, we find crudeness and imperfection in it. But even after it has been perfected we find degeneracies. *Technik* safeguards against degeneracy and protects us from it. Any degeneration of art into what is frivolous or trifling would contradict the action of the Holy Spirit. But since it is a degeneration, it cannot be said to discredit the art itself; it serves instead to caution us to seek rules. At this point, then, we must try to organize the field of practical theology as a whole.

THE SCOPE AND ORGANIZATION OF PRACTICAL THEOLOGY

The only way to organize the field is to divide it, and the question becomes, what sort of principle can we follow? We can first refer back to our definition of practical theology, and in light of it look at the purpose of practical theology. As I have said, *Technik* is to order and to guide specific actions in the Christian church which relate to its conditions and events. Thus we must first ask if we can distinguish the diversity of actions in the Christian church into separate types. Like every other ordered human association, the Christian church is an organic whole. When we view it as such, we find two sorts of activities. Every organic whole has a life-unity. When one acts upon this unity, one acts upon the whole. But every organic whole is also a complex of individual parts. When one acts upon these parts, one acts upon the whole only indirectly, insofar as the part belongs to the whole. Thus there are two sorts of influences, which can be distinguished as a general influence and a local influence. This distinction, too, is only relative, however. We will begin by discussing the concept of a local influence.

Those who direct their influence upon one individual organic part of the Christian church (the smallest organic part of which is a congregation, which in turn is a whole itself) are exerting a local influence. What makes a congregation a Christian congregation, that is, what constitutes its life-unity, is the same as that which constitutes the life-unity of the church as a whole. Thus action upon a congregation is always general in character, for one can act upon it only by seeking to strengthen the power of the spirit within it. Nonetheless, the immediate object of the action is an individual part of the church, and to this extent we can distinguish it from a general influence.

At the other extreme, when one acts to correct Christian knowledge and to strengthen the Christian sense, intending to do so in the most public way without definite limits, as we do in our writings, the activity is not local in character. It is altogether general and is aimed directly at the whole. It will nonetheless be concerned with one part of the church directly. If our activity depends on the use of language, for example, we will be more effective when our text is written in the living language of the church than when it is a translation. Indeed, even if we consider the most universal language, that of science, we find that it is limited to only a distinct sector of the church, and for this reason the activity will not be general but local in character, though in a secondary sense. The two sorts of activity can always be distinguished, even though the distinction always remains relative. It is on this basis alone that practical theology is to be divided. Indeed, this has always been done, although in treatments of the field more diligence has been given to the one part than to the other. In order to make the distinction as sharp as possible, we will let the smallest unit of the church [the congregation] serve as the organic norm for a local influence, and we can therefore say that local influence refers to activity directed toward a Christian congregation, or what we call *church service*.

A general activity, one that is directed toward the church as a whole, is more difficult to define and to hold on to. The more we direct our activity toward the whole itself, the more fragmentary our activity becomes, because the whole is never given definitively but breaks down into its particular parts. The Christian church as a unified whole is nowhere to be found. The most that is found is an individual church community. Activity in the Catholic church, for example, which is one particular unified whole, can to this extent be general. It is more difficult to identify any general activity in the Evangelical church because this church lacks any external unity. Its unity depends on something merely internal—on the [doctrinal] unity vested in its confession [of faith]. We do not find anything that we can regard as an organ of the church with respect to its doctrine. The only unified wholes are the churches of the various states, and the only way to exercise any general activity is to act upon one of these organs. These organs guide the church as a whole, and to act upon them is to participate in leadership of the whole. We therefore call leadership of the whole "church government." Inasmuch as we divide practical theology on the basis of the distinction between activities that are more general and those that are more specific, we can encompass the field within these two parts.

We must make it clear that this distinction too is only relative, however. Lying beyond church government are activities which are even more general, and more diffuse. The activity of an author of theological science is one example. We have to include this activity within church government, even though strictly speaking it is quite different. But its aim is to influence the [church as a] whole, and if the activity succeeds, it will result in an influence on the whole. The activity of authors who deal with spirituality is another matter, because although the external form of the activity is the same, the activity is not included in church government because it results only in an influence on individuals. Thus we can see that the [boundaries separating] the areas can break down and that there are transitions between them. The division remains valid nonetheless, and we can add: the more definite the distinction, the more definite the rules can be.

Several remarks must still be added to what has already been said. The first definition that we gave had already led us to the concept of art. But we have not yet said what sort of art is meant, and the division we have come to seems to make an answer to this question even more difficult. What we separate out into church service and church government is very much one and the same with respect to the church. How it can be one and the same with respect to art will not be immediately evident. In church service the various branches of what we call art in the strict sense of the world—for example, oratory, poetry, painting, architecture—occur in a variety of situations. In such instances we can easily figure out how to arrive at specific rules for applying these arts to particular tasks.

But what of church government? We have characterized it broadly as a general influence on a whole that is itself in turn something delimited. The first thing we encounter as an object toward which to direct our activity is the organization of the society itself. Let us refer back, then, to our definition, which stated that the use of practical theology presupposes impulses for action aroused by events in the church, and apply it to church government. Thus it is customary in church history to distinguish between the *fata secunda* [favorable conditions] and the *fata adversa* [unfavorable or adverse conditions] of the church—a distinction that results in a very imperfect treatment of church history but which we can adopt here. Favorable or unfavorable events call forth rules by which changes can best be made. That is, these events will call forth activity, and the discipline of practical theology is to teach us how to undertake that activity in a correct way. But what sort of art is involved here? The analogue is not hard to find. With the same right as people speak of the art of politics, we can speak of the art of church government.

But it seems that we must stretch rather far to say that the art applied in church service and church government is identical. We will have to make a small detour here if we are to avoid discounting the unity of the discipline even more than it is.

If we ask what we mean by art, we find it no easy task to answer with an explanation that would hold true for every use of the term. But such is the fate of all terms of such scope. If we look at what is an especially prominent area, that of the fine arts, we find that it always borders on and is distinguished from what we call mechanical activities, though we use the term "art" for them, too. We are in search of a *Technik,* rules for carrying out correctly something that is already known to be a task. What role do rules play in the fine arts and in the mechanical arts? In the mechanical arts, the rules themselves dictate their application. This is not the case in the fine arts. Even completely disregarding the question of creativity, for rules do not produce creativity, we still have to say that when creativity is present, the rules do not assure how creativity is to be applied. This remains a matter of special talent. In purely mechanical activities, the rule itself already dictates its application, and only the precision and the certainty of the application remain at issue. Every mechanical activity goes back to calculation; the rules and their application are given at the same time. Thus for each of the

Introduction to the Field 107

arts we have to figure out the specific relationship between rules and the task.

If we compare these two fields [the art of church government and the fine arts] which seem so remote from each other, we find that arts such as the art of politics, the art of education, and therefore the art of church government have one characteristic in common with the fine arts. [The study of] politics may establish many rules about the internal and external relations of the nation, but the rules do not insure that they will be applied correctly. It is for this reason that we say a statesman is also an artist. If we relate the art of church government to this analogy, we are led to the same result: it shares one characteristic in common with the fine arts. In the field of fine arts, every work is truly pure art in that it has no purpose beyond itself; it is to be nothing other than a presentation. Can the same be said of a work in the field of practical theology as well? If a church hymn is flawless in its presentation, we say that it has fulfilled its purpose. But in the case of religious discourse, we do not say that it has fulfilled its purpose merely because it has satisfied all of the rules of art. We demand that it produce a certain effect. In the case of true arts, this is a secondary consideration, for the only effect desired is that of a delight in the presentation. If delight in the presentation is the only effect produced by a religious discourse, we say that it has failed to achieve its purpose. We demand that it have an effect on the emotions, an effect which is distinct from delight in the presentation. We demand an effect that is active, that passes on the impulse present in the speaker to those who are addressed.

The question then becomes, How do the rules that are established by and result from practical theology relate to the goal that is to be reached? How does activity relate to the results that are to be produced? There is a strong temptation to speak of this relationship in terms of the distinction between means and ends: the result is the end; the rules are the means. This view is so obvious, so familiar to us in practical life—and church practice is so similar to practical life—that it cannot be overlooked. I mention this because the discussion that follows will show that I cannot acknowledge the view to be correct for the field of practical theology. It is the source of many errors; much of our criticism of the Catholic hierarchy, for example, is due to the fact that it considers its methods to be nothing but means to an end. At this point, then, we want to show that the view which takes means to be means to an end must be immediately qualified: the means cannot involve anything that even indirectly comes into conflict with the goal.

The true end of practical theology is church leadership in its totality—an end that is itself easily related to the true task [of maintaining and strengthening the church] as a means to an end. But many actions undertaken as means for completing a particular task could by their very nature weaken the strength of the Christian principle or dissolve the church community. In some situations, for example, people may think that the best way to maintain peace in the church is to suspend inquiry into certain issues. They foresee that to continue inquiry when emotions are so heated would lead to conflict. *Any suspension of inquiry, however, is a suppression of the scientific spirit, and will prove harmful to the [church as a] whole.*

Likewise, an action which may be quite useful in dealing with an individual in the church may inevitably destroy the Christian spirit in the [community as a] whole. For this reason we are cautioned not to employ any means which is in contradiction to the end in its totality or any method which, generally considered, contradicts the two elements of the scientific disposition, for what is in contradiction to these things has to be obstructive, and the effect of the activity can be harmful. If we examine practical theology in a critical way so that it can serve as a standard by which to evaluate the methods that we employ in the church, then it is very significant that we have gained this critical canon: *Do not employ any method that contradicts the spirit common to the church and science or weakens the Christian principle or destroys the common spirit of the church.*

If we again take up our line of inquiry, returning to it from this point, we find that we do not have to view rules as means at all. That is, as soon as one thinks of such a distinction as that between means and ends, it follows that the means have to fall completely outside the end. It thus becomes possible that the means may include something in conflict with the end. If we ask in what sphere does the overall task of practical theology fall and in what sphere do possible means fall, we can only conclude that the means used in practical theology fall in the same sphere. The particular tasks are merely small parts of the total end.

By "means" we always understand something that is willed not for its own sake but for the sake of some end. In so doing, we presuppose that an end can be isolated and that some human actions fall outside the end. Of course, we know that we can isolate an end only in a relative sense. If we assume that all ends are interconnected, and that this interconnection is morality, then we immediately conclude that we should not employ any means that are contrary to the Idea of morality for any end. The Idea of morality is the overall goal to which all goals are related as parts. But we will also have to say that, relatively speaking, it is always possible to isolate a certain sphere of ends, and thus means falling outside of this sphere would have to be applied. That this point does not hold for everything in the same way will be obvious to everyone: some ends are easily isolated; others are isolated only with difficulty. The more closely an end is connected to the overall end, the more difficult it is to isolate it. From this viewpoint we must therefore ask, Of what sort is the end of practical theology? This crucial question, of course, should not be introduced in a discussion of something that we have noted in advance to be secondary matter. But this is not actually the case. We intend to give up the notion of correlating means and ends and to stick to our main task, which is to unify the various tasks in this field.

I now propose this thesis: All of the specific tasks related to church leadership are part of what the Greeks called *psychologia*. I refer to the Greek expression directly because it is at home there. The term is easily translated as "guidance of souls," but is more at home in the Greek language. The reason it is not as much at home among us is because of the separation of public and private life, which occurred at almost the same time as our language was formed. The activities of private life seemed so different from those of public life that there was no need to subsume the two under one concept. The education of children, for example, is obviously guidance of souls; it is directed toward developing the soul. Politics, too, is nothing other than guidance of the souls, for however its subject matter is viewed or its goal defined, we are dealing with aims that can be reached only by free action and by movement, and so come about only by an influence on the soul. But we must concede that our way of life offers little occasion for subsuming church and state under one concept. The state, too, can pass laws about the education of children, and parents should pay heed to the network of legal relationships into which they enter, but although these two spheres are certainly related, they are not unified in a common point.

If we must grant that the church has been a mediating agent for bringing together the private and the public realms, then we must admit that the concept of guidance of souls has always been present in the church, even if there has not been a clear awareness of it. In modern times this point is cited in defense of something about which people usually complain: the dominance of a hierarchy over politics. The completely fallen realm of politics, it is said, must by necessity be made subject to a hierarchy. I mention this only by way of acknowledging a presupposition among us, not in order to justify it. What is aimed at is what we call edification, and the task is to call forth this psychic condition; the task is therefore a guidance of souls.

Taking a broader view of the church as a great body, we must say this. Even when we look at what is most evident to us, that is, the relationship between the religious community and the state, and we think "something here should be changed," then in and of itself this represents nothing other than an acknowledgment of a certain relationship between the two, and a direction of the will to act in accord with this acknowledgment. Everything is based on a common insight and a well-founded common decision. If a new situation is to arise, it will have to be produced, and this is a guidance of souls. The task of practical theology is to set forth the rules by which this change can take place, and none of its rules should fall outside the sphere of a guidance of souls. By the same token, any art used in practical theology should be a guidance of souls—a movement, an impulse to be strengthened, weakened, awakened, or eliminated. In this way church government and church service converge, and we can clearly see that they are so closely related that they can cross over into each other. We will first discuss church government, the need for which gives rise to a guidance of souls.

If the church is persecuted, we want to see to it that the persecution ceases; if there is conflict with heretics, that the truth is known; if disbelief threatens the church, that the disbelief itself end. What does all of this mean? Nothing other than that we want every human to become a quite good and perfect Christian. If this goal were achieved, this branch of the guidance of souls would no longer be necessary. But when we look at the social order by itself, we see that each person does as he or she pleases, not wanting to do anything else. The guidance of souls that makes up church government will be necessary as long as some individuals lack self-knowledge and purity of will. Were we to pursue every other art and, forgetting about church government, say that we want everyone to act in such a way that all those around us will accept Christianity, then church government would not be necessary. But this would mean that instead of intending to reach the goal we have set for ourselves, we would be intending to dissolve the society and to eliminate any activity which relates to particular occasions.

Both rules have been present in the church, and when they are, there is no practical theology. The first constitutes *separatism,* which seeks to dissolve the external form of the society; the second is *quietism,* which makes no response to particular occasions or to other persons. Both have always been repudiated by the general voice of the Christian church. We have now identified the good roots of both, but we have to admit that so far as history shows, they can be found only in small and particularized groups, and not in the church as a whole. Whenever people direct their efforts to large-scale endeavors, they must begin on all fronts simultaneously. So long as the final point of perfect Christianity has not yet been reached, an intelligible, ruled, deliberative procedure that responds to individual occasions which have a bearing on the condition of the church as a whole is indispensable.

As for *church service,* it too aims at the *guidance of souls.* In every other field of endeavor, we can say that it is beneficial to produce particular effects by the use of certain means. If at any given moment it is important that something happen that can be brought about only by human powers, I must employ all of my eloquence in order to make my convictions felt. Is this true of religion also? Can we produce results that are true and not merely illusory here by applying certain rules?

If we assume that faith is awakened through preaching, we can also assume that it can be strengthened by the same means. A sermon should be the work of the Spirit, and in this sense we need only be concerned that the Spirit is truly alive. But there is something between the preacher and those in whom faith is to be awakened—*the purity of the medium.* The latter should understand the former rightly, and this can be brought about only by this part of practical theology, for a preacher's effectiveness depends on the purity of the presentation. Thus we should not shy away from rules. The same thing holds for every activity in the field of practical theology. Guidance of souls is necessary for the same reasons that error is possible, and therefore rules about our procedures will always be necessary.

We have already seen how much is to be expected from the use of practical theology. So, too, we have now gained something else— the insight that the rules and the *Technik* with which we are dealing are indispensable. They are unable, however, to produce any activity itself, and as *rules of art* they are always in a certain sense underdetermined. The person who applies the rules needs something else in order to guarantee that they are applied correctly. What must be added if the rules are to achieve their purpose?

There is a special talent required for every true art, and the question therefore becomes whether a special talent is required for practical theology as well. In other fields of endeavor, talent makes the artist. Rules are of use only to those who already have talent, for otherwise what they produce will be merely the appearance of art. As soon as one investigates any of the arts, one finds in it something that extends throughout the entire course of the operation but cannot be found in the rules. Technical directions, however many there may be, cannot make anyone into an artist. All the rules may be applied correctly, but upon its completion the work still falls short of the Idea of a work of art. Of course, some errors are violations of the rules, and one can say that the creator of such a work should have followed the rules. But some works are unsuccessful in the sense that one must say that anyone who would make such a thing is not cut out to be an artist. Do we have to presuppose some such talent for the field of practical theology?

It is difficult to answer the questions for both church service and church government at the same time. In the case of church service, we are more accustomed than is proper to think of the minister as an orator, and the question then becomes whether the orator, or the minister as an orator, has to have a special talent. Even if such a talent were present, it would still not produce a perfect minister, for the task of ministry requires even more than talent. We have defined all of the art in the field of practical theology by the general term "guidance of souls." In church service, then, we can assume that a guidance of souls would have to result if the talent distinctive to the orator were correctly applied. Likewise, if the art applied in church government is in any way similar to the art of politics, it is that it too is a guidance of souls, for it concerns itself with bringing forth or preventing the actions of other persons. But church government also requires more than oratorical talent if we are to avoid the conclusion that church service and church government are utterly different. We must try to identify their point of unity.

This much is certain: Were we to assume that oratorical talent were the special talent required for church service, and were we to ask if one becomes an outstanding preacher by possessing great talent and by following the rules of oratory, we would have to conclude that the answer is no. For all of us will recall that unless this

Introduction to the Field 113

talent is accompanied by a living conviction about what is said to a Christian congregation, and an interest in it, no amount of talent could produce an outstanding preacher. The objection could be raised that it is precisely the art of orators to make others believe things that they themselves do not believe, and therefore they can evoke the faith which they themselves lack. Thus everything would depend on possessing this art and applying it with virtuosity. But this argument is only an apparent truth. Although political orators, for example, may not be true friends of their country, they may have great power to sway an audience to whatever or for whatever they want by presenting it as something beneficial. But can such persons impart the true patriotism which they themselves lack? We will have to say no, for in the first example the task is merely that of bringing forth some momentary excitement, and in the second it is that of enlivening a vital power that is the same every time it is demonstrated. In such a case the task demands the truth.

So, too, church service has to do not with producing momentary effects but with nurturing the *Christian disposition,* and it would be a great evil to think that those who lack this disposition could evoke it in others by the use of art. The devil, of course, is said to be able to disguise himself as an angel of light. But it is wrong to say that the devil could produce the same effects as the angel of light. When we deal with the communication of a spiritual principle, we must say that only those who have it can communicate it. Thus the talent of the orator becomes less significant. But given this conclusion, we should then ask whether it is possible to communicate the Christian disposition in its power and fullness without any art. Yes, it is possible, but if its effect is to be certain and pure, art will always have to be introduced as an aid.

Let us examine church government by looking at civil society as its analogue. We find in civil society something often called the art of politics or even political wisdom, that is, a talent for correctly identifying the relationships among the various factors in any situation and for making use of whatever is appropriate to produce a desired result from the situation. If we do consider this to be a talent, we may want to say that there is a "churchly wisdom" which is the talent in church government. But even if this wisdom were applied with perfect virtuosity, it would still not produce any lasting results unless it were accompanied by the fullness of a Christian disposition. It remains bound to what is given in the particular moment, and thus true, living zeal would be more effective than wisdom.

We have now identified two sorts of art, but they cannot accomplish anything unless a common element underlies them both. Rules alone do not make an artist. Before an artist can emerge there must be *the truth and purity of a Christian disposition,* in addition to rules. With respect to a Christian disposition, however, we cannot speak of distinct levels but only of gradations of more or less. Thus we will have to say that no one can be completely excluded from making an effect upon the church. The only one who might be excluded would be the one in whom the Christian disposition were the weakest. By pointing to this extreme case, we can see why it is that the stronger power can be said to be the basis for spontaneity, and the weaker power can be limited to receptivity.

But if we examine the matter more closely in order to identify the principles by which to divide the aim of practical theology into its natural parts and to set forth the way to proceed, we must take into account the relationship between those from whom such an effect is to come and those upon whom such an effect is to be produced. Of course, since the relationships are infinitely varied, we will have to mark off certain boundaries. This much is obvious: If every member of the community were perfectly equal to every other with respect to their relationship to the [community as a] whole, there could not be any leadership activity at all. There would be only cooperation, and since any influences would be merely accidental, and minimal, no rules could be given for them. *Inequality* is once again shown to be necessary. But inequality may also be too great, and in that case, too, leadership activity becomes impossible. That is, when the spirit dwells so exclusively in the one part of the community that it is altogether absent in the other, leadership activity governed by rules becomes impossible. The task becomes that of first overcoming the absence of the spirit. But there are no rules by which to do this; it has to result from a free influence on another.

Taking this inequality within the community as our point of departure, we will say that ongoing leadership activity becomes possible only when the inequality develops into a distinction, that is, when two different classes are somehow organized in the community. The one class will be comprised of those who are productive; the other, those who are receptive. These classes are found in the smallest units of the Christian church from the very beginning. Whenever a Christian society has formed, this sort of distinction has formed as well, establishing itself in certain common aspects of life within the gathering. Therefore we certainly find that leadership was always present, even though it was not of such a sort as to lead to a practical theology. Within the narrow confines of life within such a community, where everyone is subject to essentially the same experiences, every activity arises more from the immediate moment, and hence no thought can be given to a theory.

We have already shown that the positive disciplines generally could not emerge until Christianity had grown to a larger size. If each congregation that had formed had remained an isolated whole unto itself, one of the preconditions for practical theology would certainly have been absent. We must therefore say that practical theology depends not only on the size of the church but on the bonds within the large association. Perhaps, however, someone will say that although this is a condition necessary for theology in general, practical theology seems to be an exception. It could be said that leadership activity may take place within a number of individual congregations, even though it does not extend over all of them, and thus a theory could be established. We cannot deny this point. But we will still have to admit that no theory can appear until leadership activity has appeared, for if we ask what leads a congregation to understand the inequality among its members in terms of a distinction between two classes, we will have to say that it does so only when the inequality is the sort produced within a large body.

We can cite one society that illustrates the point very well, the Society of Quakers or the Friends. It has spread widely, but it exists only in the form of separate congregations and is comprised only of persons of the same class. They make it something of a principle to pay no heed to social distinctions. The natural outcome is that those at the extremes of social differentiation do not take membership in this society. One finds no social outcasts and few from the privileged classes. The society is very extensive, but its character is such that the inequality within it is minimal. In such a case, a theory of practical theology is inconceivable. A theory develops only in societies which have considerable historical continuity and which contain within themselves a certain degree of inequality. The form that this distinction among the members takes is that one group embodies the common spirit in a productive manner; the other group, more in a receptive manner. If the inequality within the society remains unformed, the only relationships that develop are those of one individual to another, and no theory can be established. Therefore, a theory of practical theology presupposes this distinction, which is found in all organic communities, as well as in civil society itself.

We must now define the character of the religious community with more specificity, and ask what makes one group within it more productive and the other receptive. If the distinction is rooted in an actual inequality, then this inequality must be related to the character of the community itself. Since its character is formed by piety and religious awareness, and since the community cannot survive except through mutual interchange, the inequality must be nothing other than that one group has more to give, and can give more, to the other through communication. The fact that some have more to give is the distinction that is to be overcome. Therefore the inequality develops into a distinction permitting those who are productive to exert a certain influence on the others only for the purpose of overcoming this inequality and producing an equal possession by means of mutual communication.

In calling the one group receptive, we are not saying that it is passive. On the contrary, we ascribe activity to this group, too. Its activity must of course be tested by the Idea, in living reflection. But if we then go on to ask what gives direction to a general inclination to exert an influence by means of communication, we will have to answer that it is the condition of the other group. And if we ask how the one group gains its knowledge of the needs of the other, we will say that we must assume that this group engages in some self-[initiated] activity that expresses its needs. The more pointed this expression is, the more it can serve to give direction to the activity of others. Thus we can sum up the matter as follows: the one group communicates, and the other group does not merely receive, but acts upon the other by manifesting its needs; it calls them forth to action. This is what is meant by the concept of a living circulation.

Although we might wish to stop at this point, we are faced with a consideration of an altogether peculiar sort. If we think of this process—for which practical theology is to establish a theory—as fully perfect, we must say that the equalization [between the two groups] will come about as quickly as possible. The more perfect the process, the more swift the exchange. And if we think of the process as perfect, we must say that leadership activity would cease. We can think of ongoing leadership activity only if the distinction among the members of the community reappears again and again, and this occurs because of the change of generations.

Thus everyone acts and is acted upon; practical theology becomes an art for everyone. But we must try to be more specific. Whenever an art is applied, there must be specific forms: what is formless will be artless as well. The extremes converge here. Specific forms of art are most often found in church service, and here art is most at home; in church government, it is less so. But since church government must also have a church society as its object, forms of art will be present here, too.

Some actions upon the community as a whole are by their very nature unlimited, and no particular art can be specified for them. This is true of every activity that is intended to have a completely unlimited effect upon the church. Both the particular form and the rule of art disappear. A congregation composed of families is the smallest, yet still organized, whole on which an effect can be made. Family circumstances, however, are quite varied. Therefore activity in this smallest area is formless; no form of art can be specified. The region within which the most specific forms can be identified lies between these extremes. Thus we are led back to the point that particular effects can be produced only on a particular whole.

We find that some wholes are constituted more externally, while others are constituted more internally, qualitatively, as are, for example, the church parties in Christendom, which must be viewed as distinctive modifications of Christianity that are more or less perfect. Likewise, we have to deal with such a difference as long as the Evangelical and Catholic churches remain distinct. The one church can produce indeterminate effects upon the other, either its individual members or generally, but effects that are properly included within practical theology can be produced only within one and the same church.

Are effects in these two churches produced by the same rules; that is, *can there be the same practical theology for Evangelical as well as Catholic theologians?* This question can be answered in different ways. There can be one that is indifferent; another, purely polemical. These answers will be contradictory: the former will maintain that the rules are the same in every respect; the latter will deny that they are at all the same. Neither answer is any more true than the other, for both are based on false principles. The truth lies [somewhere] between the two, but it is difficult to express. Some rules are the same for both churches, but if one goes into specifics, one finds that the different principles [of the churches] become apparent. But we cannot specify where the difference and identity begin and end. The formula is theoretically correct, but because in practice we cannot be more specific, we will have to limit the validity of our practical theology to the Evangelical church.

We can never point to any place in either church service or church government where the difference between the two churches would not be reflected by necessity in actual activity. Since the churches have completely different principles about the relationship of the church to the state, as well as about the relationship of the two churches to one another, even the first principles of church government will have to be different. With respect to church service, the relationship between the clergy and the laity in our church differs from that in the Catholic church, and Evangelical ministers have completely different resources at their disposal because they can count on greater familiarity with scripture and value the realm of tradition differently. The elements are so different that rules about their use will have to be worked out differently. It would be futile, then, for us to write first a general practical theology and then a special one. It is more appropriate for us to limit our discussion to the Evangelical church at the outset.

THE ORDER OF TREATMENT

We have divided the field of practical theology into the theory of church government and the theory of church service. With which part should we begin? The two are so different that obviously we have to begin with one, and ask if it relates to the other as a prerequisite and if the relationship cannot be reversed. If we assume that the church is an organic whole, then we already know the answer, and the only thing left to do is to state it with clarity, for in an organic whole all of its parts are mutually conditioning. We can naturally expect, then, that each of the two parts of practical theology will be conditioned by the other. Hence no particular order of treatment can be said to be given by necessity.

If we begin with the theory of church government, we have to presuppose something that only church service can provide. There cannot be any church government unless the church is united as an association of many Christian congregations. A unified church presupposes the existence of individual communities which must be maintained by means of church service and renewed throughout the change of generations by means of education that depends on church service. If we begin with church service, we find that it cannot be completely independent and free [of church government] unless it were directed toward absolutely autonomous congregations. Both together, church service and church government, can be undertaken only inasmuch as much of church service is conditioned by church government, and if we were to begin with church service, we would have to presuppose these conditions. We find ourselves in the same predicament no matter where we begin.

At this point we have to refer back to the origins of the Christian church. How could church service or church government have ever arisen if each presupposes the other? [The answer is that] both were united in the work of the apostles. To be sure, the initial activity of the apostles was that of church service. It was actually by the work of the apostles, not Christ, that the church and its congregations were begun. Alongside the apostles were disciples of Christ, who had already been joined and brought together externally, though not perfectly. They formed a congregation, and the apostles, who allowed the disciples to establish themselves in Jerusalem, devoted themselves exclusively to church service. Yet inasmuch as the apostles felt the desire to extend Christianity and founded congregations which were brought into association with those already in existence, thereby modifying them, they engaged in church government. Only by this means, that is, by referring to the unity of the two [church service and church government] in the same point, can we account for their origin. Since [as matters now stand] the two are separate, it does not matter which we begin with. Our decision must be based on subjective, external reasons; there cannot be anything definitive about it.

Church service and church government are connected at two points. First, both are directed toward the same object, the church, no matter whether one sets out from the Idea of the larger community or from the satisfaction of the individual's religious needs which are immediately fulfilled within the local congregation. Since there is a lively interchange in the sphere of religion, both must be brought into correspondence, and this occurs only by means of interchange within the church as a whole. Moreover, the well-being of the whole consists only of the well-being of its individual members.

Second, a religious interest and a scientific spirit are necessary for both those who participate in leadership of the church as a whole and those who engage in church service. Much can be done about the internal organization of the church and its relationship to the state on the basis of a practical approach and a sound understanding of life. But without a theory, progress comes about more or less at random. A scientific spirit, however, is necessary in order to develop a theory and put it into operation in actual activity, and beneficial progress is altogether dependent upon it. Rather than respond to a call to justify why we make church government one of the main parts of practical theology, we have to ask how it has come about that this part has been overlooked.

We find that the Catholic church places the exercise of the church office [of ministry] as well as church leadership in the hands of the clergy. There the connection between church service and church government is manifest by the very nature of the case. But the role of science is less prominent in that church than in ours, and this is true of both parts of practical theology as well. Among Catholics the exercise of the office of ministry depends less on speaking than on working with symbols. The same is true of pastoral care, because everything is done according to tradition and here, too, science recedes. Thus here, too, science is less significant. Catholic clergy are trained in a number of experiential learning sessions. As for higher leadership of the church, here, too, tradition rules—a sort of secret doctrine in the Roman curia, because church authorities are in constant opposition to political authorities. But the reason that the distinction between church government and church service seems so great in the Catholic church is because of its sharp distinction not only between the clergy and the laity but between the higher and the lower clergy as well. Church government is placed in the hands of the higher clergy; church service, in the hands of the lower.

The opposite is the case in the Evangelical church. There are no sharp distinctions between the clergy and the laity or among the clergy themselves. Such distinctions are perhaps found in an episcopal system, but where this system is actually maintained, evangelical purity is lost. The activities of the clergy and laity are quite different, for leadership of the church as a whole rests less in the hands of the clergy than in those of secular persons. It is for this reason that a theory of church government is supposedly non-theological: politicians, not theologians, govern the church. But no one can claim that this arrangement belongs to the essence of the Evangelical church. A counterthrust against a hierarchical constitution is certainly present, but the fact of the matter is that there are some whose role in church leadership falls more on the side of science and others whose role falls more on the side of politics. We should view the clerical and temporal authorities as equals with respect to their leadership over church affairs; otherwise the clergy would in effect become subordinates. The theory that is applied in church government therefore has both a more theological side in keeping with the concept of the church and a political side in keeping with the concept of the state. Of course, we must say that the continuance of theology itself is dependent on activities of church leadership over the whole. For if there were no overall context, then given our presupposition, there would be no theology either. But it also follows that if leadership of the church overall is carried out poorly, the result will be an influence harmful to theology, and thus on church service as well, for it is dependent upon theology.

As we have already said, the two parts of practical theology often cross over upon each other. We take church service to include everything pertaining to carrying out the office of ministry. But it seems that principles for these activities have to be presented in the theory of church government so that legislation about the office of ministry orders things correctly. Leadership of church affairs is chiefly concerned with the relationship of the clergy to the state and the interrelationships among the churches themselves. The main point is that *unless the legislation is defended in public opinion, it will be weak,* especially in a spiritual sense. Public opinion is to be formed by the exercise of the office of ministry. Therefore, it seems as though the theory of church government must be developed so that the clergy will come to a correct understanding of how to direct public opinion. A minister's service in the congregation therefore requires a correct view of church government. It would be completely improper for secular authorities alone to try to regulate the form of public worship and the relationships among its individual elements. The two parts of practical theology are so essentially and organically connected that the theory of the one must relate to the theory of the other. Which of the two should come first?

There are two considerations that suggest that one part has a certain priority over the other. First, for any given individual, administration of the congregation always comes first, and participation in leadership over the church [as a whole] comes afterward. Second, in keeping with the spirit of the Evangelical church, it seems altogether essential that the larger unit be considered relatively less important. Individual congregations were the first thing to develop in the Evangelical church, and the unity of the church as a whole— as an external organization—has not yet developed anywhere. The unity extending throughout the Evangelical church is only internal. We must grant priority to what is most prominent in our church.

One other matter must be discussed before we proceed to deal with church service or church government in particular. Since the concept of the church is common to both parts, we must set forth this concept in a common way. Its external feature is very easily identified: it is baptism which defines a person as a member of the Christian church, and implicit in baptism is relationship to Christ. If we examine the meaning of baptism, and the relationship to Christ implicit in it, we find that it sets forth a certain direction for the human spirit in all of its undertakings. Christ presents us with an archetype that we are to approximate, and the words of Christ set out a pattern for human thinking and acting. On the assumption that there is agreement about this basis (Christ), *the Christian church becomes the totality of those who endeavor to approximate this archetype in their common life.* Thus the rule which serves to insure that activities in the Christian church take place correctly is: Whatever promotes an approximation to Christ is correct; whatever hinders this approximation is false.

The content of this rule still remains problematic of course. With regard to the two parts of practical theology, the question becomes how and by what means does the office of ministry promote such an approximation and, likewise, how can leadership of the church as a whole promote or hinder it. We note that Protestantism is opposed to Catholicism, and this brings with it a different conception of the question.

The primary activity of those holding the office of ministry in the Catholic church has to do with the sacrament, even with respect to the influence that they exert on the lives of individuals. Connected to this central point is the set of symbolic actions that take place in corporate worship. These alone give this church its distinctive character.

In the Evangelical church, it is preaching, the exposition of the divine Word, rather than symbolic action that emerges as decisive in corporate worship. Thus no one can dispute that guidance of souls is carried out in our church especially by means of speaking. For this reason some have been led to the view that the Christian church is actually an educational institution. I will have to admit that this view seems to be one-sided. Since it is linked only to an opposition to the Catholic church, it seems to slight the common element expressive of the essence of the Christian church as a whole. When do those who hold the office of ministry engage in teaching? They first do so in their catechetical instruction to youth. But those who receive instruction are not yet full members of the Christian church.

Introduction to the Field

Thus teaching seems to be more a preparatory work than the essence of the ministerial office. Moreover, catechetical instruction is by no means the same as preaching, for a sermon should not be a lecture. We therefore have no right to say that the church is an educational institution.

What sort of theory of church government results if one starts out with the view that the church is an educational institution? [A wish] that people not be ignorant about general human affairs is not an interest peculiar to the church but a common interest, indeed, an interest of civil society. For this reason there arises the inclination to merge the two [church and society], and because the will of the state must be that people not be ignorant of anything beneficial to them, it is natural to say that if there are any educational institutions in the state, they must have originated in it and been adopted by it. Thus the more often the church is viewed as an educational institution, the more often it is viewed as a political institution, and its ministers as public teachers. This institution's relationship to the original concept of the church is totally lost.

Preaching is certainly central to the Evangelical church. But should every expression and communication of thought be considered teaching? Whenever teaching takes places, it aims at a certain completeness, that is, an overview and summary—otherwise, it would not be teaching. But we do not find any such thing in the church. Even though preaching in the church may be handled in such a way that it aims at doctrinal completeness, it reaches its aim merely accidentally, through what comes about in human life. The effect sought by those who hold the office of ministry is not that the Christian congregation will be instructed, but that it will be edified; that is, an effect on the congregation that moves from the feeling to the will. Thus we must conclude that a view of the Christian church as an educational institution is a one-sided view that must be considered as the cause of all errors. Along with it comes a tendency to make the church subservient to the state. And if we think of the role that religious music and poetry play in the church, we see that teaching has disappeared completely.

From a purely historical perspective, we are led to say that the Christian church has arisen from the effects and activities of Christ. *What was the will of Christ?* How wonderful it would be if we could proceed from this point. Some have said that Christ was a teacher and that he wanted to do nothing but teach, that his disciples were like him, and that the continuance of this institution is an educational institution. Others have asked why Christ would have spoken of a kingdom if he had envisioned merely an educational institution. The kingdom conveys the Idea of a corporate body. It is implicit in what we have already said that these two extreme views—that the church is an educational institution and that the church is a corporate body—are in and of themselves dangerous, for when we start with either view, the object disappears under our hands. People who are taught differently become in a sense different. Thus we would be left only to carry out what the politicians tell us to do. Were we to set out from the other extreme and maintain that we want to build a church that is a corporate body so perfect that no aspect of corporate life is excluded, we would be led into conflict with the state. Thus the object for which we are establishing a theory disappears before us.

If we ask what the church into which we want to introduce our theory really is, we will have to say that it is something more than an educational institution. It is truly, although imperfectly, a corporate body. We must therefore take care lest the church degenerate into a mere educational institution or turn into a corporate body of such a sort that it comes into conflict with the state. We must sketch out in advance, although in only broad and general terms, what must be viewed as the basic element common to both parts of practical theology.

What should we regard as the principle governing all leadership activity in the church? We must take into account the present division between Protestantism and Roman Catholicism. If the Christian church were an educational institution, could the theory of leadership activity be more or less the same for Protestants and Roman Catholics? We would have to say no, because in the Catholic church the clergy—that is, one particular segment of the society as a whole—is in full control of doctrine. Hence this sector within the Catholic church forms the church in the strict sense of the word, and is usually referred to as the church. The laity are a "middle rank" between those who belong to the church and those who are outside it. With respect to their own self-activity they are outside of the church; with respect to their thoughts and actions, they are passive. They are in the church insofar as they allow themselves to follow its guidance, and this is the decisive reason for their passive obedience. Those of us in the Evangelical church regard doctrine as common property, and do not ascribe any passive obedience to the laity. On the contrary, we maintain that their obedience should arise out of [personal] conviction.

Can the theory of leadership be the same for these two churches, assuming that the church is viewed as a corporate body? Certainly not. The Catholic church is actually a corporate body extending across a number of civil corporate bodies; it is a corporate body outside of civil corporate bodies and encompasses everything. In the Evangelical church, however, there is no leadership activity extending over the church as a whole; every activity that is or develops into leadership activity is limited to the boundaries of a single corporate body. We must therefore identify where the Evangelical church stands with regard to these two views, and then attempt on that basis to identify the principle of practical theology as a whole.

In order to be satisfactory for the entire Evangelical church, the formula we come to must neither omit anything essential to this church nor include anything equally applicable to another church. We need not give any thought to distinguishing the Evangelical church from any other church except the Roman Catholic. If we could sum up the difference between these two churches by means of a general formula, we would at the same time be able to express the distinctiveness of the Evangelical church. Doctrine, whether about beliefs or morality, is always a personal matter, and we must take the Idea of community as our starting point. The church community must by necessity have a certain order. This order, which we call its constitution, expresses the character of the church in the most definitive sense possible. The differing constitutions found in the Christian church are due to differences in the way the clergy and the laity are related in these communities. These differences had already emerged very early in history, and the Evangelical church's decision to deny to its clergy what the Catholic church grants to its clergy must be considered one of the foundational acts by which the Evangelical church was formed.

The Evangelical church affirms an equality among its members: each and every individual is granted personal responsibility. The Catholic church holds individuals responsible only for their obedience, and not even that. The clergy is to blame if it allows any disobedience to set in. In the Evangelical church, by contrast, the clergy is viewed as a body that is formed out of the community as a whole. They therefore have no authority except that granted to them by the community. *Ministerium verbi* [the ministry of the Word] does not refer to a distinct class, but to a distinct function in the church, which is given over to certain individuals—this point is essential in the Evangelical church. We can therefore say that *the Evangelical church is a community of Christian life devoted to the independent exercise of Christianity.* By this means we can distinguish between the Evangelical church and the Catholic church as definitively as possible. We presuppose, of course, that no temporal claim is made within the community. In the Evangelical church, the institution of a public office of ministry—to which the visibility of its corporate life is linked—is established without endangering the independence of any individual.

Practical theology is to provide a theory by which the Evangelical church can be maintained as this sort of community, insofar as its maintenance can be insured by deliberative and free actions. Thus the question becomes, How can we identify the particular form to be given to each of the two parts of practical theology? What should be not only preserved but also perfected is the independent Christian life of each individual in the church, and this is the task that falls to church service, which deals with individuals directly. The essential function of church government has to do with individuals only in a derivative way, in the sense that it assigns them certain functions. Its chief concern is to form the corporate life in such a way as to insure that Christian life will be preserved. The theory of church service answers the question of how the independent exercise of Christianity is maintained and strengthened by means of all the actions that the church directs toward individuals. The theory of church government answers the question of how the independent exercise of Christianity can be maintained and strengthened by means of the actions that the church directs upon the organized communities themselves. This question involves not merely the styles of communicating within the church itself but the external relations of the church, and therefore the church's relationship to civil society especially.

We have tentatively concluded that the validity of what is set forth in our practical theology will be limited to the Evangelical church alone. But it does not follow that this restriction will apply to every point equally—this we can anticipate in advance, for it is always true. The distinctiveness of a historical phenomenon is not expressed equally in each of its constitutive elements, and does not influence every action equally. Had we decided to proceed by focusing on the relationship between the Evangelical church and the Catholic church, we would have had to begin by answering the question of the extent to which our statements are valid for the Roman church and the extent to which they are based on what is distinctive to our church or what is common within Christianity. As it is, we merely raise this question in a general way and leave it open for reflection.